OXFORD*mode*

Across the Barricades

Joan Lingard

adapted by

David Ian Neville

OXFORD
UNIVERSITY PRESS

OXFORD
UNIVERSITY PRESS

Great Clarendon Street, Oxford OX2 6DP

Oxford University Press is a department of the University of Oxford.
It furthers the University's objective of excellence in research, scholarship,
and education by publishing worldwide in

Oxford   New York

Auckland   Cape Town   Dar es Salaam   Hong Kong   Karachi
Kuala Lumpur   Madrid   Melbourne   Mexico City   Nairobi
New Delhi   Shanghai   Taipei   Toronto

With offices in

Argentina   Austria   Brazil   Chile   Czech Republic   France   Greece
Guatemala   Hungary   Italy   Japan   Poland   Portugal   Singapore
South Korea   Switzerland   Thailand   Turkey   Ukraine   Vietnam

Oxford is a registered trade mark of Oxford University Press
in the UK and in certain other countries

This adaptation of **Across the Barricades** © David Ian Neville

Activity section © Jenny Roberts 2003

The moral rights of the author have been asserted

Database right Oxford University Press (maker)

This edition First published 2003

British Library Cataloguing in Publication Data

Data available

ISBN: 978 019 832079 1

10 9 8 7 6

Typeset by Fakenham Photosetting, Fakenham, Norfolk

Printed and bound by Bell and Bain Ltd, Glasgow

Acknowledgements
The Publisher would like to thank the following for permission to
reproduce photographs:
Corbis/Bryn Colton/Assignments Photographers: p 71; Magnum Photos:
pages 21, 30, 49, 66.
Map by Oxford Design and Illustrators.
All other artwork is by Peter Melnyczuk.
Cover image: Corbis/Hulton Deutsch Collection

Extract from *Across the Barricades* by Joan Lingard (Hamish Hamilton, 1972),
copyright © Joan Lingard 1972, reprinted by permission of Penguin
Books Ltd.

'Mixed Marriage – Running the gauntlet of disapproval' by Martin O'Hagan,
Fortnight, June 1986, reprinted by permission of Marie O'Hagan and *Fortnight*
Magazine.

Contents

General Introduction

With a fresh, modern look, this classroom-friendly series boasts an exciting range of authors – from Pratchett to Chaucer – whose works have been expertly adapted by such well-known and popular writers as Philip Pullman and David Calcutt. We have also divided the titles available (see page 96) into subcategories – Oxford *Classic Playscripts* and Oxford *Modern Playscripts* – to make it even easier for you to think about titles, and periods, you wish to study.

Many teachers use Oxford *Playscripts* to study the format, style, and structure of playscripts with their students; for speaking and listening assignments; to initiate discussion of relevant issues in class; to meet the Drama objectives of the Framework; as an introduction to the novel of the same title; and to introduce the less able or willing to pre-1914 literature.

At the back of each Oxford *Playscript*, you will find a brand new Activity section, which not only addresses the points above, but also features close text analysis, and activities that provide support for underachieving readers and act as a springboard for personal writing. Furthermore, the new Activity sections now match precisely the Framework Objectives for Teaching English at Key Stage 3; a chart mapping the Objectives – and the activities that cover them – can be found at the beginning of each section.

Many schools will simply read through the play in class with no staging at all, and the Activity sections have been written with this in mind, with individual activities ranging from debates and designing campaign posters to writing extra scenes or converting parts of the original novels into playscript form.

For those of you, however, who do wish to take to the stage, we have included, where necessary, 'A Note on Staging' – a section dedicated to suggesting ways of staging the play, as well as examining the props and sets you may wish to use.

Above all, we hope you will enjoy using Oxford *Playscripts*, be it on the stage or in the classroom.

Conflict in Ireland

Across the Barricades is a story of survival – the survival of friendship against all the odds. It is set in Belfast, Northern Ireland, in the 1970s, at a time of terrible violence and conflict. The majority of people in Northern Ireland are Protestant, and in the 1970s most of them believed that Northern Ireland should be part of the United Kingdom, ruled by Parliament in London, with the Queen as its head of state. At the same time, other people living in Northern Ireland (mainly Catholics) believed they should be part of the independent Irish Republic, which is made up of the provinces in southern Ireland.

The history of Northern Ireland is long and complex, but the violence and hatred between the two sides reached a peak during the late 1960s and 1970s. (The activity on page 76 should help you understand the situation more clearly.) During the conflict, both sides resorted to terrorism, thousands of people were killed, and thousands more lived in fear.

This story is about two people, Sadie Jackson and Kevin McCoy. Although they live near each other, there is a huge gulf between them – the gulf of prejudice, bitterness, and fear. Although their story is set in Northern Ireland, it could take place anywhere in the world where people are divided by conflict and terror.

What the Author Says

When I wrote the first book about Catholic Kevin and Protestant Sadie growing up in Belfast – *The Twelfth Day of July*, which precedes *Across the Barricades* – my aim was to make it as balanced as possible. I did not want to be on one side or the other. I wanted to be for the Protestants and for the Catholics, seeing the good and the bad points in both. I wanted to write a book that would make my readers think about prejudice and the way we tend to divide up society into 'us' and 'them'.

In order to create a balance, I decided to alternate chapters, moving between the Protestant and Catholic communities so that they would occupy similar space in the book. I then balanced my characters by giving Kevin a sister, Brede, the same age as Sadie, and Sadie a brother, Tommy, the same age as Kevin. The action I set in the few days leading up to the Twelfth of July, the day when the Protestants celebrate the victory of King William of Orange (otherwise known as King Billy) over the Catholics at the Battle of the Boyne. That took place in 1690. Memories are long in Ireland.

At the start of The Twelfth Day of July, Kevin and Sadie are outright enemies; by the end of it, they have come to have some respect for one another and there is the beginning of an attraction between them. They have also come to challenge some of the prejudices and fears of their upbringing. I had no

thoughts of writing a sequel, but when I was working on the last chapter I realised that I had on my hands two characters who were going to refuse to lie down. I had to find out what happened to them next! So I went on to write *Across the Barricades*, and subsequently *Into Exile*, *A Proper Place*, and *Hostages to Fortune*. Thus their story became a quintet and spanned seven – very important and crucial – years of their lives.

Joan Lingard

A Note on Staging

Costumes and Props

Props you may need include:

Sadie:	old photographs; a bag; a comb; a jacket or coat.
Mr Jackson:	an evening newspaper.
Kevin:	bits of scrap; a single rose (to give to Sadie); bandages, including a wrist sling; a suitcase.
Brian:	an old army rifle; a balaclava.
Brian's friend:	a balaclava
Uncle Albert:	an old coat and hat.
Brede:	2 cups of coffee.
Mr Blake:	a pipe; a tray of tea and biscuits; a cup of tea.
plus:	picnic things; a blanket.

The Stage

The scenes take place in various parts of Belfast and in Sadie and Kevin's homes. The first impression of the set should be of either a wasteland or junk yard filled with assorted objects including an old armchair, a table, old tyres, old boxes, etc. Throughout the play these objects can be used as props for the various scenes. Among the junk there is a broken or twisted barrier, which gives the impression of dividing the acting area. It need not be in the middle, or divide the acting area into two equal sections, it can be moved around throughout the play, but is a constant element of division both physically and symbolically. During the play, 'key' areas of the acting area will represent 'Sadie's home and street' and 'Kevin's home and street'. The play can be performed with an audience on three sides of the acting area. The back of the acting area can be used for entrances and exits, but performers can also enter through the audience.

Visual Effects

You may wish to feature a number of slides showing children in Northern Ireland as part of the opening sequence of the play. When the play was first performed by the Tag Theatre

Company, touring schools, it was decided not to use slide projection. Stage directions referring to the use of slides have been left in the script as an option.

Sound Effects

The play opens with Sadie looking through some old photographs. Ideally, until Sadie puts the photographs away on page 13, all speech should be recorded, as if part of a radio interview.

You may wish to open your play with music. At several other key moments in the play, the stage directions indicate that music is desirable. Choose the kind of music you think most appropriate. In the original production specially commissioned music was used effectively throughout as indicated.

For Scene Twelve, you may wish to consider recordings of police and fire engine sirens.

Characters

Sadie Jackson	A sixteen-and-a-half year old Protestant living in Belfast. At the start of the play she is working in a department store in the centre of Belfast. She is energetic, good humoured and has a determined and stubborn streak in her character.
Kevin McCoy	A seventeen year old Catholic. **Kevin** lives a few streets away from **Sadie**. He works in Dan Kelly's scrapyard. He is hard working and easy going, but like **Sadie** he is also stubborn. Both **Kevin** and **Sadie** have decided not to follow the 'crowd' and neither is easily led.
Brede McCoy	**Kevin's** younger sister. When they were younger, **Kevin** and his friends were involved in street fights with the Protestant kids who lived nearby, but **Brede** would never get involved. She was 'the only peace loving one amongst them'. On one occasion, while innocently watching a street fight, she got badly injured and nearly died.
Tommy Jackson	**Sadie's** brother. He works in the shipyards like his father. But unlike his father he refuses to join the Orange Lodge. After taking part in the street fight in which **Brede McCoy** nearly died, **Tommy** has refused to march on the Twelfth of July. For a time when he was younger, **Tommy** and **Sadie** became friends with **Kevin** and **Brede**. But after a while they grew apart because it was too difficult for them to see each other.
Mr Jackson	**Sadie's** father.
Mrs Jackson	**Sadie's** mother.
Uncle Albert	**Kevin's** uncle. **Albert** is **Kevin's** father's brother. **Albert** is one of life's optimists. Despite the Troubles and the fact that he never has a proper job, and that his old car never works properly, he can always manage a smile and a joke.
Brian Rafferty	**Brian** has been a friend of **Kevin's** since they were both kids. But now they are growing apart. Some say that **Brian** is getting mixed up with the Provisional IRA.
Kate Kelly	**Kate** is **Brede's** friend. **Kate** is keen on **Kevin** and they are friends, but they are not going out with each other – at least that's how **Kevin** sees it.

Linda Mullet	**Linda** lives next door to **Sadie** and they have been friends for years, but now **Sadie** has little time for **Linda**.
Mrs Mullet	**Linda's** mum is a 'good' neighbour to **Mrs Jackson** – good at borrowing things, good at keeping up with all the local gossip, and good at blaming **Sadie** for being a bad influence on **Linda**.
Mr Mullet	**Linda's** dad and a friend of **Mr Jackson**.
Mr Blake	**Mr Blake** is a retired schoolteacher who used to teach at **Sadie's** school. He lives in the quiet suburbs of Belfast.
Steve	A friend of **Linda Mullet's**.

Newsreader
Teenager 1
Teenager 2   in **Sadie's** street/crowd
Soldier 1
Soldier 2
Neighbours

ACROSS THE BARRICADES   CHARACTERS

SCENE 1

*Sadie enters and sits on the ground downstage right. She begins looking through a bundle of old photographs. We hear **Sadie** and **Kevin**'s voices.*

Sadie   *[Off]* We were kids then ... I was about thirteen, Kevin was ... how old were you?

Kevin   *[Off]* Fourteen ...

He clears his throat.

Sadie   Everyone round my bit was getting reading for the Twelfth Day of July★ ... Tommy, that's my brother, he was practising the flute ...

Kevin   *[Laughing]* And you were going to be a majorette!

Sadie   Don't laugh, I was serious about it then ... Anyway, the first time I met Kevin, he'd come round to our street and ... well, him and this guy, Brian, started painting over our mural of King Billy★★ ...

Kevin   We made a right mess of it ...

Sadie   Anyway we caught them red-handed and ran after them ...

Kevin   Brian got away, but I tripped over my shoelace ...

Sadie   He always says that ... it's rubbish, I pushed you to the ground ...

Kevin   Oh yeah!

Sadie   Well, anyway, that was the first time we actually spoke ... we wanted to beat each other up ...

Kevin   But being the kind generous sort of person I am, I let her go ...

★ The Twelfth of July was the date of the Battle of the Boyne in 1690, when the Protestant William of Orange defeated the Catholic armies of James II. Protestants celebrate this day with marching bands and banners.
★★ 'King Billy' is the nickname for King William of Orange.

Sadie	You mean I let you go ...
Kevin	Rubbish!
Sadie	Well, the point is, for a while we were sworn enemies ... Tommy and I went into the Catholic area to get our own back ... and it just went on and on from there ...
Kevin	Brian and I went back into the Protestant area ... it was just a game ... they made a move, we made a move ...
Sadie	But all that was years ago ... a lot of water's passed under the bridge since then, as they say ...

A 'sting' of music, such as you would hear on local radio before the news bulletin.

Newsreader	*[Off]* Loyalists have claimed responsibility for a petrol bomb attack on a Falls Road pub and the Provisional IRA have said they were behind the explosion which destroyed a supermarket in the Shankill Road. Weather in the Province will remain warm this evening, with sunny spells tomorrow throughout the day. Not too many problems reported on the roads at the moment, rush hour traffic in Belfast is flowing smoothly ... *[fade]*.

*During the report, **Sadie** has put the photographs away in her bag. She combs her hair and puts on her jacket or coat. She's leaving work.*

Sadie	*[To the audience]* It had just been a normal day. I'd been bored stiff working in the hat department, watching all these stupid women try on some really awful hats. *[Putting on a voice]* Yes, madam, that's really nice, goes lovely with your outfit – old stuck up bitches! I was glad to get out at five thirty. I'd spent the whole afternoon daydreaming and counting the minutes on the department clock, which is always five minutes slow ...

*Kevin appears behind **Sadie**.*

Kevin	*[Calling]* Sadie? ... Sadie Jackson?
Sadie	*[To the audience]* I was on my way to the bus stop, and all of a sudden I hear this fella shouting my name ... Oh, I recognized

him all right ... it's just it was a bit of a shock, know what I mean?

Kevin   Sadie? I thought it was you.

Sadie   Kevin! ... *[laughing]* Kevin McCoy!

Kevin   Well, well, haven't seen you in ages ...

Sadie   Years more like ... must be about three ...

Kevin   At least. So what you doing with yourself these days?

Sadie   You really want to know?

Kevin   Sure.

Sadie   I'm eh ... training to be a brain surgeon.

Kevin   *[Laughing]* Oh, of course, I should have guessed!

Sadie   What about you?

Kevin   Oh ... em ... the same, you know ... *[They laugh]* You fancy a cup of coffee? Have you time?

Sadie   Don't see why not.

Kevin   I know a brilliant little place round the corner does a wonderful cappuccino ...

Sadie   Oh, get you ... first of all it was coffee, now it's cappuccino!

Kevin   Well, us brain surgeons we do have sophisticated tastes.

Sadie   *[To the audience]* I could have said hello and goodbye and left it at that. It would have been easier, less trouble. But life's never that simple, is it?

Kevin   *[To the audience]* Sadie was even better looking than I thought she'd be. Like, I remember when we were kids I thought she might turn into an all-in wrestler, she wouldn't let butter melt in her mouth, I'm telling you ...

*Sadie's friend, **Linda Mullet**, enters.*

Linda   Hi Sadie, you going for the bus?

Sadie	Oh, hi Linda . . .
Linda	Well, well, who's this you're with? Don't I get an introduction? . . . Wait a minute. I've seen you before, haven't I?
Sadie	*[Sourly]* Everyone's seen him before.
Linda	No, I know the face . . .
Kevin	Yeah? I've had it for a while.
Linda	I remember you . . . You're Kevin McCoy and you live up the Falls.
Kevin	Well done, you've won the star prize!
Linda	I knew I'd seen you before.
Sadie	Well, I'm glad you won't have to sit worrying about it all the way home on the bus.
Linda	Haven't seen you for a while . . .
Kevin	You obviously don't frequent the right places, do you?
Linda	I'm not sure I'd want to. Well, Sadie, are you coming for the bus?
Sadie	Not right now, Linda, I'm staying in town.
Linda	Oh, are you then?
	She looks at **Kevin**.
	Oh well, in that case I'll leave you to it. Be seeing you, Sadie.
Sadie	No doubt.
	Linda *walks off*.
Kevin	She can't get home quick enough to spread the news.
Sadie	Let her spread what she likes.
Kevin	I was thinking . . . eh . . . if you're not in a rush, maybe we could go for a walk somewhere.
Sadie	It's a nice evening – we could take a walk up Cave Hill.

| Kevin | Good idea. |
| | *They go off.* |

● ●

SCENE 2

Sadie's house, evening. **Mrs Jackson,** *Sadie's mother, is setting the table and preparing the evening meal.* **Mr Jackson** *comes in and sits in the armchair reading the evening paper.*

Mrs Jackson	Are you going to the Lodge★ tonight, Jim?
Mr Jackson	I always go to the Lodge on a Tuesday.
Mrs Jackson	Just asking, that's all.
	Tommy comes in.
Tommy	Is tea ready yet, Ma? I'm starvin'.
Mr Jackson	You should be asking him if he's going to the Lodge.
Tommy	Aw, Dad, we've been through all that and I've told you it's not for me.
Mr Jackson	Huh!
Tommy	Are we ready to eat? I'm meant to be going out.
Mrs Jackson	Oh, it's ready all right. I'm just wondering where that sister of yours has got to. You'd think I had nothing to do but stand here slaving over a hot stove for her convenience. She's got no consideration for other people.
Tommy	Sadie would give you her last penny if you needed it.
Mrs Jackson	If she had one to give. Her pay packet's been spent before she gets it.
Mr Jackson	Come on, Aggie, let's eat. I've got to be at the Lodge for seven.
	From offstage we hear someone knocking at the door. It's **Linda.**

★ The Lodge is a meeting place for members of the Orange Order, a society set up by Protestants in the 1790s.

Linda	*[Off]* Anybody in?
	*Linda enters. **Mr Jackson** is obviously annoyed that his meal is going to be delayed even more.*
Mr Jackson	Hello Linda, did you get fed up waiting on Tommy?
Linda	Hello ... oh sorry, I didn't realize you'd still be eating.
Mr Jackson	We're a bit later tonight. You haven't seen Sadie on your travels, have you?
Linda	Well, I did actually. I saw her on my way home, but I don't think she was on her way home.
Mrs Jackson	So where was she going? She might have told us.
Linda	I don't know where she was going, but ...
Mrs Jackson	But what?
Linda	Oh nothing.
Tommy	I'll be ready in a few minutes, Linda. I was thinking we could go to the cinema ...
Mrs Jackson	What were you going to say, Linda?
Linda	*[Hesitantly]* Well ... Sadie wasn't alone.
Mr Jackson	Oh. And who was she with?
Linda	I don't know if I should tell you that.
Tommy	Maybe you shouldn't then. I'm not feeling that hungry. Come on, Linda, let's get on our way.
Mrs Jackson	Just a minute, Tommy.
Mr Jackson	I think Linda knows something we ought to know.
Linda	I don't want to cause any trouble ...
Mrs Jackson	If there's something you think we ought to know you must tell us.
Tommy	Let's go, Linda.

Mr Jackson	Well, Linda what have you got to say for yourself?
	Linda looks nervously at Tommy, but she can't stop herself from telling them about Kevin.
Linda	I suppose you've got a right to know … she was with that Catholic boy, Kevin McCoy.
Mrs Jackson	What are you talking about, Linda?
Linda	It was that boy Sadie and Tommy got mixed up with three summers ago, the one whose sister got hurt. They were waiting on a bus together.
Mr Jackson	What do you know about this, Tommy?
Tommy	Nothing. I don't see what the fuss is all about. I mean, it's not as if she's going to marry him.
Mrs Jackson	Marry him? Oh no …
Tommy	She hasn't seen him in years, Mum. There's nothing in it!
	Pause. Mrs Jackson is in a state of shock. Mr Jackson is comforting her. Linda is trying to avoid looking at Tommy. Tommy stares at her.
Tommy	I'm going to the pictures. You can come if you want.
	Tommy walks out without waiting for a reaction from Linda. Linda looks uneasily at Mr and Mrs Jackson, then follows Tommy out. Mrs Jackson begins clearing the table, her hands shaking. She is almost frantic. Mr Jackson follows her off the stage.

● ●

SCENE 3

Cave Hill, evening. Sadie and Kevin enter and sit downstage.

Sadie	It's beautiful up here, isn't it?
Kevin	I love Cave Hill. I like sitting here, looking down on the city.
Sadie	It looks so peaceful.

Kevin	It does you good to get out of the city of an evening.
Sadie	There's no one to bother you up here ...
Kevin	Does it worry you about Linda seeing us?
Sadie	It's none of her business.
Kevin	Thought she was your best friend?
Sadie	You're joking. Linda Mullet? She's just like her father, always out to cause trouble ... Don't know what our Tommy sees in her ...
Kevin	So Tommy's going around with Linda?
Sadie	She drags him all over Belfast and he pays.
Kevin	Has he got a job then?
Sadie	He works down there in the shipyards. What about you? Have you got a job?
Kevin	Aye, remember Kate Kelly, you know, Brede's friend?
Sadie	Yeah, what about her?
Kevin	I'm working in her father's scrapyard.
Sadie	Really? And does she go with the job?
Kevin	Very funny!
Sadie	She used to fancy you rotten, didn't she?
Kevin	Hm, and what about you? What are you up to these days?
Sadie	Trying to change the subject, are we? *[Laughing]* Must be some life roaming the streets looking for scrap.
Kevin	Well, some of the scrap isn't exactly what we're looking for ...
Sadie	What about all these burnt out cars and things?
Kevin	You daren't touch them. People use them ... Burnt out cars, buses, torn-up paving stones, barbed wire ... it might be scrap to you and me, but it comes in handy for building barricades ... Oh, it's fun roaming the streets of Belfast ... you see a bit of life ...

Sadie	Ah well, let's forget about all that.
Kevin	Yeah, you're right.

Pause. They look around, taking in the view.

Sadie	It's funny seeing you after all this time.
Kevin	And you ...
Sadie	I mean, after all, we only stay a few streets away from each other ...
Kevin	Yeah, but it might as well be a thousand miles.
Sadie	Remember when we first met, when we were kids ... we were sworn enemies ...
Kevin	It was a good laugh to begin with, a bit of a game right enough ... Kevin's gang, Sadie's gang ... calling each other names ... *[Shouting]* Down with the Prods!
Sadie	*[Shouting]* Down with the Micks!

As they begin to remember the past, it comes alive almost like a dream sequence.

Kevin	I remember Brian and me sneaking into the Proddie's area in the middle of the night to paint over your lot's King Billy ...
Sadie	What about when I got into your house in the middle of the night and wrote 'Down with the Pope' on the kitchen table ... it took poor Brede ages to scrape it off ...
Kevin	*[Almost to himself]* Oh, it started as a bit of fun all right ...
Sadie	*[Almost to herself, as if remembering a bad dream]* But it ended in a pitched battle ... I remember it as if it was yesterday ... the eleventh of July ... Bonfire Night ... We were on one side of the road, they were on the other ...

Music, sounds of the battle in full flight, children shouting, bin lids being bashed together, stone-throwing.

Kevin	We'd been building up to it for days ...

Sadie	We started shouting 'Down with the Micks! Down with the Pope!'.
Kevin	*[Shouting]* Down with King Billy and all the Prods!
	*At this point, other members of the cast appear, playing the parts of other kids in the 'battle'. Together with **Kevin** and **Sadie**, they mime throwing stones and shout 'Down with the Prods' etc. as though the 'battle' is actually taking place. While this is going on, **Sadie**, **Kevin**, and other members of the cast narrate what happened, their voices charged with the excitement of the battle and almost having to shout above the noise.*
Sadie	People started throwing stones, then bricks …
Teenager 1	Anything you could lay your hands on …
Teenager 2	People were going mad …
Kevin	Everyone was getting carried away with the excitement …
Sadie	Everyone except Kevin's sister Brede … she just stood there, not shouting or throwing anything, just watching …
	*By now **Brede** has appeared in the middle of the battle, but she is not involved, she just stands very still.*
Kevin	Then someone threw a brick … she tried to duck, but she wasn't quick enough …
Sadie	*[Screaming]* Brede!

Everyone freezes and for a few seconds there is silence, then other members of the cast walk off slowly, leaving Sadie and Kevin alone again.

Sadie	Brede never hurt anyone ... in fact, the only time I'd ever met her she'd been very civil to me ... I ran to help her, it was just something I had to do ...
Kevin	*[To Sadie]* I'll never forget that, you and Tommy helping Brede.
Sadie	All I remember is waiting in that hospital, with you, me, and Tommy, wondering if Brede was going to die. Brede never harmed a soul and here she was the one that comes out worst when there's trouble ...
Kevin	After that we became friends. You, me, Tommy, and Brede, when she recovered. We had some good times ... going off to the seaside at Bangor, coming up here ... we had a laugh ...
Sadie	But it all got quite difficult, you know, telling our parents we were going somewhere else ... so we grew apart and that was that, until now ...
Kevin	*[To Sadie]* We must do it again sometime ...
Sadie	What?
Kevin	Go to Bangor for the day, you and me like.
Sadie	Well, when do you want to go?
Kevin	How about Saturday?
Sadie	We'll take a picnic, make a day of it, eh?
Kevin	You're on!

Music. Sadie and Kevin exit.

• •

SCENE 4

Sadie's house, late evening. Mrs Jackson is setting out the table for breakfast; Mr Jackson comes in, back from the Lodge.

Mr Jackson	Is she back yet?
Mrs Jackson	She's up in her room.
Mr Jackson	Oh, is she now?
Mrs Jackson	How was the Lodge?
Mr Jackson	Mullet was there. He wanted to know what all this was about.
Mrs Jackson	Did he say anything to anyone?
Mr Jackson	You can't keep a thing like this quiet, it's no use pretending . . . that girl, honestly, she'll get us all into trouble.
Mrs Jackson	Jim, what are we going to do?
	Sadie comes in.
Mr Jackson	I wish I knew . . . well, well, you're home?
Sadie	I'm allowed out, amn't I?
Mrs Jackson	The whole street's talking about you, Sadie.
Sadie	Linda Mullet, she's the whole street?
Mrs Jackson	*[Whispering]* The Mullets have got connections . . .
Sadie	All I've done is go for a walk with a boy.
Mr Jackson	Well, you're not seeing him again, that's for sure, d'you hear?
Sadie	I'll see him if I want to, it's a free world.
Mr Jackson	*[Grabbing her arm]* Is that what you think? Is it?
Sadie	*[Moving away]* Look, leave me alone . . .
Mr Jackson	As long as you're under my roof, you'll do what I tell you.
Sadie	I don't need to stay under your roof. I'm sixteen, nearly seventeen. I can do what I want . . .
Mrs Jackson	Sadie, that's enough . . .
Mr Jackson	Oh, so we're independent now, are we? She's earning twenty-five quid a week and she's independent . . .

Sadie	Well, you wanted me to go on that stupid training scheme, didn't you?
Mr Jackson	Ah well, we'd soon see how far you'd get under your own steam. You've got all the ideas, haven't you? You know everything, don't you? You don't seem to realize that we're a family and what you do affects us all.
Mrs Jackson	Jim . . . calm down . . .
Mr Jackson	Next time you choose to go for a walk, you go for a walk with one of our own kind!
Sadie	*[Going]* I'm going to bed, I've had enough of this!

Sadie walks out.

Mr Jackson	*[Shouting]* Sadie! I haven't finished with you yet . . . get back in here this minute!
Mrs Jackson	Let her be, Jim. You'll only end up turning her against you.

We hear music – rebellious, rock – Mr and Mrs Jackson exit. Sadie comes back on. She begins looking through some old photographs.

Sadie	*[To the audience]* My parents? . . . Well, I suppose they were all right really . . . I mean, my father wasn't violent or anything like that, not like some of the people round our way. But he took the Lodge seriously . . . his father was a good Orangeman, so he had to keep up the tradition. He wanted Tommy to join . . . but then Brede got hurt and we just couldn't go. My parents went crazy, they didn't understand . . . we were just kids, but we were 'letting the side down' . . . My father's forever going on at Tommy to join up . . . he gets a lot of stick in work as well . . . but Tommy's not interested . . . I mean, does it make you a good Protestant to march through the streets playing a little flute?

*Sadie exits and, as the music fades, **Brian** and **Kevin** come on.*

SCENE 5

*Kevin's street, early morning. **Kevin** is busy working in Kelly's Scrapyard. **Brian Rafferty** is trying to talk to him. **Kevin** tries to get on with his work, moving different bits of scrap around.*

Brian	All I want to know, Kevin, is one thing – are you a good patriot?
Kevin	Brian, what are you going on about?
Brian	I mean, you believe in the cause, don't you?
Kevin	Of course. I'm a republican, amn't I?
Brian	*[Softer]* We have to be prepared to fight for what we believe in, don't we? I mean, you are ready to fight?
Kevin	I don't see what good it would do, to be honest.
Brian	You can't mean that?
Kevin	Look, d'you mind if we discuss all this later on? If I don't get on with my work, Kelly will have a fit.
Brian	Sure. We don't want to get on the wrong side of old man Kelly or for that matter Kate. No doubt she'll have your coffee ready for you soon . . .
Kevin	Yeah, yeah . . .
Brian	Kate was wondering where you were last night . . . in fact, we all were.
Kevin	Listen, let's get this straight, Brian . . . Kate and I are just friends, all right?
Brian	Have you told her?
Kevin	Drop it, Brian . . .
Brian	A bit touchy today . . . must have been a late night?
Kevin	Yeah, as a matter of fact it was. Now, if you don't mind . . .
Brian	Sure thing, Kevin, don't let me keep you. We'll have a good old chat later. It's important, very important. Anyway, I'd

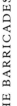

better be going myself ... things to do, people to see, know what I mean? ... See you, Kevin.

Kevin   See you later.

Brian goes off. Kevin continues moving some of the scrap around, then looks at his watch and starts to get ready to leave. His sister, Brede, arrives.

Brede   Hi, Kevin, are you finished for the day?

Kevin   Yes, I'd better get home earlier tonight or Ma'll do her nut.

Brede   Who was she, Kevin? The girl you went out with last night?

Kevin   Me? Out with a girl? Never.

Brede   Look, I wasn't born yesterday. I know you. You were in another world this morning at breakfast.

Kevin   I was tired.

Brede   Oh yeah, come on, Kevin.

Kevin   Not much goes past you, Brede.

Brede   So who was she? You can trust me ... I won't say a word to Kate.

Kevin   It's got nothing to do with Kate. We're not sworn to each other ...

Brede   Well, you know how she feels about you.

Kevin   I've never given her any cause to feel like that. Kate's got a good imagination.

Brede   I know. Come on, Kevin ... tell me ... is it someone I know?

Kevin   Someone you used to know ... a while back.

Brede   Stop playing games, you idiot.

Pause.

Kevin   She lives on the other side.

Brede   It wouldn't be Sadie Jackson, by any chance?

Pause.

It isn't?

Kevin	It is.
Brede	Are you seeing her again?
Kevin	I'm taking her to Bangor on Saturday. We're going to spend the whole day there ... have a picnic ...
Brede	Kevin, d'you think it's wise seeing her again?
Kevin	Aw, Brede ...
Brede	Look, I like Sadie, she's a nice girl, all right ... but think about it, Kevin ... think about where she lives and where you live ... should you be getting involved with each other?
Kevin	There's a lot of things nobody should be doing these days. Look I'm going to pop in and see Brian before I go home. Tell Ma I'll be back soon.

Kevin walks off.

| **Brede** | Kevin! |

Music. **Brede** *holds her position for a few seconds, then exits.*

● ●

SCENE 6

Brian's house, evening. **Kevin** *and* **Brian** *enter together.*

Brian	Kevin, I told you I had something important to talk to you about. Glad you could come round ...
Kevin	Brian, what are you going on about?
Brian	I've got something to show you ...

He closes the 'door', checks the window.

Wait until you see this, Kevin. You won't believe it ...

| **Kevin** | Don't tell me you've got your hands on a stick of dynamite? |
| **Brian** | Oh no, this is much better than dynamite ... |

He pulls an old box out from under his 'bed' or some other hiding place, opens it up, and unwraps an old army rifle.

This is something that is going to come in very useful, very useful indeed ... Ever seen one of them before?

Kevin   Where do you get that?

Brian   Oh, it's pretty old, but it still works ... It's quite a heavy old thing ... feel it.

Kevin takes the rifle, holds it, then quickly gives it back to Brian, almost as if touching it has soiled his hands.

Brian   Oh, it's powerful all right ... and there's five rounds of ammunition to go with it ...

Kevin   You're crazy! You're out of your head, Brian.

Brian   *[Angrily]* And how exactly do you work that out?

Kevin   You can't keep that thing here – the Brits could be round searching the neighbourhood any time.

Brian   *[Smiling]* Well, that's just it, Kevin, I was thinking of hiding it somewhere ... somewhere like Ould Kelly's scrapyard.

Kevin   You've got to be kiddin'. The old man would have a fit.

Brian   He doesn't need to know anything about it. You could find a good place to hide it.

Kevin   I don't want anything to do with guns, Brian. It's madness.

Brian   That's not the way you once talked. There was a time when you were full of fighting to get the six counties back from the English. A united Ireland! Up the rebels! What's happened to all that?

Kevin	I was younger then.
Brian	Some excuse that!
Kevin	There's enough people getting killed. I want nothing to do with it.
Brian	You're a coward, that's your trouble.
Kevin	*[Grabbing Brian]* Take that back!
Brian	Give me one good reason.
Kevin	Brede almost died because of all the trouble, or don't you remember?
Brian	*[Breaking away]* Well, she's all right now, isn't she?
Kevin	That's not the point. Look, where did you get that thing from anyway?
Brian	Oh, that's right, I'm sure to tell you.
Kevin	You think I'd split on you? Don't be stupid, Brian.
Brian	Look, you want one Ireland, don't you?
Kevin	*[Pointing to the rifle]* Not with that, I don't.
Brian	There's no other way. Why don't you join us?
Kevin	I'm not afraid of fighting if I see a need for it, but I'm not for people dying.
Brian	But it's the enemy that'll die.
Kevin	You're not such an eejit as to believe that. If there's bullets flying, your mother or mine could be standing in the road.
Brian	So you won't be one of us?
Kevin	*[Moving away]* It's not a game any more.
Brian	Traitor!
Kevin	Call me what you like, Brian. There's dozens of Catholics who aren't one of you either, and don't you forget that!

| Brian | If you let on about this, you know what'll happen. |
| Kevin | Just be careful what you do with that thing . . . you might end up blowing your own head off. |

*Brian points the rifle at **Kevin**.*

| Brian | Hold it right there, Kevin! *[Laughing]* Scared? |
| Kevin | I told you, it's not a game any more . . . |

*They both stand there very still for a few seconds. **Brian's** finger is on the trigger . . . he clicks the trigger, nothing happens . . . he laughs.*

| Brian | That got you going, didn't it? |
| Kevin | You're pathetic, Rafferty. You're really pathetic! |

*Kevin pushes past him and walks off. **Brian** follows. We see pictures on the screen of Northern Ireland, soldiers on duty, IRA members with dark glasses and balaclavas at funerals, firing rifles into the air . . . perhaps ending with a street scene with a body lying dead and men with rifles in the background . . . army, RUC, IRA, UDA – it's difficult to tell who they are.*

Or, alternatively, we hear a 'sting' of music and then the following news bulletin.

Newsreader	*[Off]* Police and army units are today carrying out a house to house search after one man was shot dead and another two men were seriously injured in an incident outside a bar in West Belfast late last night. In another incident, city centre streets were cleared with apparently only minutes to spare before a car bomb caused serious damage to buildings in the area. Police received an anonymous tip off, but as yet no organization has claimed responsibility for the device. Weather prospects for the weekend look good with clear skies and several hours of sunshine forecast for Saturday ... *[fade]*.

● ●

SCENE 7

	Bangor, Saturday. The sound of the sea, seagulls, wind. **Sadie** *and* **Kevin** *are in the middle of a picnic.*
Sadie	It's good to be out of Belfast, right enough ...
Kevin	I love it here, breathing in the fresh air and letting your thoughts drift out to sea. Ever been in a boat, Sadie?
Sadie	Only one of those rowing boats you rent for half an hour.
Kevin	*[Laughing]* One day I'll take you out in a boat and row you all the way to Scotland. Would you like that?
Sadie	When do you want to go?
Kevin	You would too, wouldn't you?
Sadie	You know me, I'm ready for anything.
	She offers him another sandwich.
	Here ... grab another one ...
Kevin	Thanks. You've made enough to feed an army.
Sadie	I was up at the crack of dawn making them – couldn't let my Ma see me, could I?
Kevin	Aye, well, there's a few in my street would be having a heart attack if they could see me now.

Sadie	Wonder what your friend Brian would think?
Kevin	I don't know and I don't care.
Sadie	What's he up to these days?
Kevin	This and that ... let's forget about your street and mine.
Sadie	Good idea. Want an apple? I brought two ...
Kevin	*[Taking apple]* You're very domesticated, aren't you?
Sadie	Not really, I just like my grub.
Kevin	*[Laughing]* Sadie, you've done us proud with this little feast.
Sadie	Well, all the fresh air, it gives you an appetite ...
Kevin	It's so peaceful here, don't you think? It's like we've got the whole world to ourselves.
Sadie	Wouldn't it be nice if we did?
Kevin	Just you and me and all this.
Sadie	Plus some food.
Kevin	*[Laughing]* Of course.
Sadie	Funny we should get on so well together.
Kevin	Why d'you say that?
Sadie	Well, you know what I mean, with so many things against it.
Kevin	Only one. And that doesn't seem to matter.
Sadie	No. Not when it's just the two of us together.
Kevin	Does it bother you when we're not?
Sadie	I don't know ... I find it odd when I think of you going to things like ... well, like confession.
Kevin	It's just part of my religion.
Sadie	Would you confess to the priest that you were going out with a Protestant girl?

Kevin	There's no law against it. It's not a mortal sin.
Sadie	I hate the word 'sin'. They're always going on about the word 'sin'. Don't you resent the power the priests have over you?
Kevin	They don't have much power.
Sadie	'Course they do.
Kevin	Rubbish. You know nothing about it.
Sadie	And these statues and things. I mean, honestly . . . I don't know how you can bring yourself to pray to them.
Kevin	What about your lot? Worshipping a silly old Dutchman dead these three hundred years.★
Sadie	We don't worship him. Never have.
Kevin	*[Standing up]* Ah, for God's sake! King Billy on his white horse. Long live King Billy! Keep the Micks down!
Sadie	If there were more of you than there was of us, you'd soon keep us down.
Kevin	So you're afraid, that's what it is!
	He laughs and moves away.
Sadie	Rubbish.
Kevin	You're all afraid.
Sadie	You're no better than the rest of them, Kevin McCoy. I hate you!
	Kevin turns his back on her and stands very still.
Sadie	*[To the audience]* At that moment I did hate him . . . I felt miserable, I felt so alone . . . I wondered if my father was right – were all Catholics the same?
Kevin	*[To the audience]* I walked away. I kept walking . . . I was furious with Sadie. I couldn't believe she was still talking about Catholics in the same old way . . . It's funny – when you have

★ Kevin is talking about William of Orange, a Protestant King of England.

an argument, you just respond automatically. You meet each attack with a counter-attack, you say things you don't always mean, there's no time to think ... Was Sadie just like all the other Protestants?

Sadie	*[To the audience]* It started to rain ... our picnic was ruined. I just sat there, I couldn't move. I wanted to catch pneumonia and die and make Kevin feel guilty ...

*Pause. Music. **Sadie** sits all huddled up and looking miserable. After a while, **Kevin** walks up behind her, kneels down, and puts his arms round her. The music fades.*

Kevin	Sadie?
Sadie	Oh, you gave me a fright ...
Kevin	No better than the rest of them, am I?
Sadie	Kevin, I didn't mean it.
Kevin	It was all pretty silly, I'm sorry.
Sadie	So am I. Thanks for coming back.
Kevin	Did you think I was just going to leave you sitting all alone on the sands? Come on, let's go and find some shelter.

They move and sit on the other side of the acting area.

Sadie	There's something really special about Bangor. I don't know what, I just love being here ...
Kevin	It's a sort of escape, isn't it? Just think, we've spent the whole day here with no one to bother us ...
Sadie	It's safe.
Kevin	It's been a good day right enough ...
Sadie	I don't want to go home.
Kevin	Neither do I, but I think we'd better get on our way. It's after half past ten.
Sadie	*[Jumping to her feet]* Oh, Kevin! Come on, we'd better run for it.

They both make a mad dash across the stage, but they arrive too late and watch the last bus move off in the distance.

Sadie   *[Worried]* Ah Kevin, I told you we'd end up missing the last bus ...

Kevin   Not to worry, Sadie. We'll hitch. Someone's bound to give us a lift.

Sadie   At this time of night, are you kidding?

Kevin   There's nothing to worry about, just stick out your thumb and hope for the best!

Sadie thinks about it for a few seconds, and then with a smile on her face she sticks out her thumb and starts hitching. Kevin smiles.

Sadie   How am I doing?

Kevin   You've got the wrist action, it's just a pity there aren't any cars going by!

They both laugh.

Sadie   I think we'll be stuck here all night.

Kevin   No, look, there's a car coming.

They both stick their thumbs out and watch several cars go racing by. This happens a few times. Gradually it becomes more frustrating. Kevin mouths obscenities at the speeding cars. Sadie laughs.

Kevin   *[Calling after a car]* I hope all your wheels fall off ...

Sadie   *[Sarcastic]* Not to worry, Kevin, we'll get a lift ...

Kevin   *[To the audience]* And we did ... Suddenly this old banger stopped, it was like an answer to a prayer ... But my ecstasy did not last long - I recognized the driver ...

By now, Kevin's Uncle Albert has appeared and begins ushering them into his 'car'. The 'car' is made out of old seats that are part of the set. Uncle Albert is wearing an old coat and hat and looks like he has a permanent supply of Guinness. He is an eternal optimist and good humoured.

Albert	Well, well, this is an unexpected pleasure. Jump aboard, my boy, you and the young lady. Make yourself comfortable!
Kevin	Sadie, this is my Uncle Albert . . .
Sadie	Oh, hello.
Kevin	Uncle Albert, meet Sadie.
Albert	Oh, you've been keeping her well hidden, Kevin. *[Laughing]* Oh, you're a right lad and no mistake!
Kevin	*[To the audience]* It was embarrassing enough being caught with a girl, but a Protestant? I was sure he was going to catch us out any minute . . .
Albert	That's the stuff. Now, you can just sit there in the back and have a wee cuddle! I promise not to look!
Kevin	Just keep your eyes on the road, Uncle Albert.
Albert	Why? Does it do tricks?

He roars with laughter.

Now, you two might be wondering what I'm doing out here at this time of night. Well, to be honest, I went to see a man about a dog! I'm telling the God's honest truth here . . . it was the nicest greyhound I've seen in a long time, beautiful beast . . . Oh, I was tempted, but the missus would throw me out if I brought it back home . . .

Sadie	*[To the audience]* I liked Kevin's uncle, he was a good laugh, but I was dreading him asking me too much about myself . . .
Albert	So, where do you live then, Sadie?
Sadie	*[Off guard]* Em . . . eh . . . not far from Kevin.
Albert	Funny, I've never seen you before. I'd have remembered . . . Oh, you know how to pick them, Kevin!
Kevin	Don't listen to him, Sadie, he's full of smooth talk.
Sadie	Well, now I know where you get it from.

36

Albert	*[Laughing and turning round]* Oh, that's a good one! Ah, that's what I like ... she's more than a match for you, Kevin!
Kevin	Keep your eyes on the road, Uncle.
	Albert swerves violently, narrowly missing another car.
Albert	*[Shouting at the other driver]* Hey you! Can you not watch where you're going! You eejit! *[Changing his tone]* You must bring Sadie round to meet the wife sometime ...
	Sadie and Kevin exchange glances and laugh.
Sadie	*[Whispering to Kevin]* This is going to be a very eventful journey, I can tell ... *[To Albert]* How far are we from Belfast, Mr McCoy?
Albert	Oh about five miles, not far to go now.
Kevin	Uncle Albert, I don't like to worry you, but there's steam pouring out of the engine ...
Albert	*[Breaking hard]* Oh no, this is all I need and me with guests aboard! All right, everyone out!
	They all get out and Albert mimes opening the 'bonnet'. Albert starts trying to wave the smoke away, Kevin looks in the engine to see what the problem is.
Albert	Oh, my poor little car's taken a nasty turn! Kevin, what am I going to do?
Kevin	It looks like the thermostat has gone. You won't get it fixed at this time of night. We'll need to leave it and walk home ...
Albert	Leave it? Mercy me, they'll have the wheels off it before dawn ... Oh well, I'll just need to get someone out to fix it tomorrow. Honestly Sadie, it's the first time my wee car's let me down like this ...
Kevin	*[Laughing]* Don't believe a word of it, Sadie.
Albert	Ah well, it won't take us long to get to Belfast, anyway. We'll have a wee song to help us on our way ...

Sadie	Oh, that's a good idea . . .
	They link arms and start walking. **Albert** *starts singing and they join in.*
Albert	*[Starts singing]* Oh Danny Boy, the pipes are calling . . . From glen to glen and down the mountain side . . .
	Albert *changes mid-song to 'The Soldier's Song'.* **Kevin** *and* **Sadie** *join in,* **Sadie** *almost before she realizes what she's singing.*
Sadie	*[To the audience]* I couldn't believe it. To my own amazement, I was joining in singing rebel songs. My father would have had heart failure if he's heard me . . . but we soon stopped singing . . .
Kevin	*[To the audience]* We were stopped and questioned by some British soldiers. An Army patrol car had been blown up . . . the driver was killed . . .
Sadie	I feel sick. Why do people do these things?
Albert	Oh, it's terrible right enough, but if they will come over here, they have to expect trouble.
Sadie	But the reason they're over here is . . .
Kevin	Sadie!
Albert	Don't get me wrong, Sadie, I'm not for people getting killed. Some of these soldiers are just boys . . . I don't know why we can't get a little bit of peace. Oh, here's me talking of peace and if I'm not home in a few minutes, my missus will be starting World War Three! *[Laughing]* No doubt Kevin'll want you to himself from here on . . .
Kevin	Goodnight, Uncle Albert.
Sadie	Goodnight.
Albert	*[Going]* See you soon I hope, eh Sadie? You get him to bring you round for tea! Night then!
	He goes off.
Sadie	He's all right, your Uncle Albert, isn't he?

Kevin	Oh, he's a good-natured soul, but a terrible husband!
Sadie	*[Smiling]* Kevin, I think you should leave me here. I'll make my own way home . . .
Kevin	Aw, don't worry. I'll walk you to the end of your street . . .
Sadie	I do worry.
Kevin	It's been a lovely day, Sadie.
Sadie	Well, we must do it again and again . . .
Kevin	And again . . .

*They stand holding hands and looking into each other's eyes. They are about to kiss when **Mr Jackson, Mr Mullet,** and **Tommy** appear behind them.*

● ●

SCENE 8

*Near **Sadie's** street, 2 a.m.*

Mr Jackson	And what time of night is this to be wandering the streets?
Kevin	I'm sorry if you've been worried about Sadie, Mr Jackson. We went to Bangor and missed the last bus . . .
Sadie	And then we got a lift from Kevin's uncle and his car broke down . . .
Tommy	I told you there would be a simple reason for it, Dad.
Mr Jackson	Simple? That's not what I call it. We've been searching for hours looking for you . . .
Mr Mullet	The whole street's been right upset and our Linda's nearly up the wall with worrying.
Sadie	Well, she'll just need to get down again, won't she!
Mr Mullet	The cheek of it . . .
Mr Jackson	Your mother's in a terrible state. She'll be at the doctor's in the morning . . .

Sadie	Aw, she's always at the doctor's ...
Mr Jackson	*[Going for her]* Why, you little ...
Sadie	*[Jumping clear]* All right, all right ... I'm coming home now anyway, but I'm not going to be marched up the street as if I was being taken to jail.
Mr Mullet	Jail would be too good for you. *[To Mr Jackson]* Sorry, Jim, but there's times a man must speak his mind. We've nearly been round the bend these last few hours thinking of all the things that might have happened to you.
Sadie	Oh, did you think the Micks had got hold of me and tarred and feathered me?★
Kevin	*[Under his breath]* Sadie!
Mr Mullet	I wouldn't put anything past that lot.
Kevin	Sadie, I'll be seeing you, OK?
Mr Jackson	You just hold your horses, young fella, I'm not finished with you yet.
Tommy	Oh, come on, let's go home to bed. We've found Sadie and that's the main thing.
Mr Jackson	That's not the main thing at all. You two go home. I've got some unfinished business with this Mick.
Tommy	Da, you're not going to start fighting.
Mr Jackson	You don't seem to care who your sister's roaming around with till all hours of the night, but I do!
Sadie	What do you want to fight Kevin for? He didn't force me to go with him ...
Kevin	I don't want to fight anyone, Mr Jackson.

★ Tarring and feathering involves smearing a person with tar and then covering him/her with feathers. It was used by Republicans as a method of 'punishing' or frightening people.

Mr Mullet	No, 'cause you're probably too yellow! You lot are all the same!
Tommy	For heaven's sake, let's go home.
	Kevin grabs Mr Mullet by the collar. Mullet is taken off guard – he's not really too keen on doing the fighting himself.
Kevin	Oh, you think we're yellow, do you? If you were my own age, I'd let you have it, but I don't pick on old men!
Mr Jackson	Why you . . .
	He grabs at Kevin, pushing Mullet out of the way.
	By the time I'm finished with you, you won't dare come near my daughter again . . .
Sadie	*[Pushing in between her father and Kevin]* If you want to fight Kevin, you'll have to take me on first!
Kevin	I don't need you to fight my battles, Sadie.
Mr Jackson	I'm going to break every bone in your body, McCoy!
	Everyone is struggling. Tommy gets in between his father and Kevin and holds his father back.
Tommy	*[Almost screaming]* Are you crazy? Break it up! If this goes on any longer, we'll have half the neighbourhood out on the streets. There's a mob gathering already up the road. We'll have a riot on our hands in a minute! Kevin, you'd best get out of here fast.
Sadie	Tommy's right. Goodnight, Kevin. *[Panicking]* I said goodnight, Kevin!
Kevin	OK, OK . . . goodnight, Sadie, Tommy . . .
	He looks at Mr Jackson.
	Goodnight.
	He walks away to the other side of the acting area.
Mr Jackson	*[Shouting]* If I see you near my daughter again, I'll kill you!

Tommy	*[Leading his father off]* All right, Da ... that's enough. Let's go.
Mr Mullet	Tommy's right, Jim. Let's leave it be for now.

Tommy leads his father away, Mr Jackson still shouting at Kevin. Mullet follows them. Just before they go off, they freeze: Mr Jackson is looking back at Kevin, threatening him, and Tommy is trying to restrain him. Kevin, now at the other side of the acting area, has his back to them. Sadie moves away from her father.

| Sadie | *[To the audience]* I've never seen my father so angry. Through the anger and coldness in his face, I could see he was frightened. He wasn't frightened of Kevin, it was more what he represented. That night, my father became a stranger to me. |

Mr Jackson, Tommy, and Mullet leave the stage, then Sadie follows them.

| Kevin | *[To the audience]* I was lucky to get away before anyone else joined in. Sadie and I had arranged to meet again the next day by the River Lagan, but after the little dust-up with her father I thought she might not want to risk it. My most immediate problem was trying to get home in one piece ... |

Sound of an explosion, gunfire, shouting etc. A soldier comes running on.

Soldier	*[Shouting]* Get down on the ground, son! You want to get killed?
Kevin	*[Obeying]* What in the names's going on?
Soldier	Have you seen anyone running past you?
Kevin	I haven't seen anything.
Soldier	Aye, and if you had, you wouldn't be saying! *[Going]* You keep your head down for the next few minutes until you get an all clear ...

Kevin	Oh sure, anything you say!
	*The **soldier** runs off. **Brian Rafferty** creeps up behind **Kevin** and puts a finger to his neck as if it was a gun ...*
Brian	It's all go tonight, eh Kevin?
Kevin	*[Turning round]* Brian! What are you doing creeping up on me like that?
Brian	*[Laughing]* You've missed all the action. Doyle's Bar got hit by the Prods. But don't worry, they're going to pay for this. They'd burn us out to the last man if we let them.
Kevin	We do a bit of burning ourselves.
Brian	I don't like the sound of that talk.
Kevin	What good does burning things do? I'm sick of fires.
Brian	So you take yourself off to Bangor for the day?
Kevin	How do you know that?
Brian	Your Uncle Albert's got a loose tongue. He told me all about your little trip to the seaside with your little blonde girl called Sadie.
Kevin	So what?
Brian	Think I'm daft? Only thing he didn't tell me, probably 'cause he didn't have the sense to know, was your little blonde girl was a Prod!
Kevin	It's none of your business.
Brian	I remember Sadie all right, a fine little Loyalist!
Kevin	You won't tell me what to do, Rafferty, so don't even think of it.
Brian	No? Oh, well, we'll see ... *[Laughing]* Take care going home, Kevin, these are dangerous times!
	__Brian__ goes off quickly. Music.

River Lagan, Sunday evening. **Kevin** *is still onstage from the previous scene.*

Kevin *[To the audience]* Belfast is a really beautiful city. We've got all these parks: Dixon Park, Barnett Park, Clement Wilson Park ... Don't ask me who Clement Wilson was, I haven't got a clue ... We've got the Botanic Gardens ... we even have a rose festival every July ... So if we're not planting bombs, we're planting flowers ... It's a very romantic city, believe me!

Sadie *joins* **Kevin.**

Sadie *[To the audience]* On Sunday night, Kevin and I met by the River Lagan as arranged. We were both a bit shaken by the confrontation with my father ...

Kevin *[Handing* **Sadie** *a single rose]* Here ...

Sadie *[Smelling it]* Very nice.

Kevin *[Joking]* Does your mother know you're out?

Sadie *[Laughing]* I'm always out. I hate being stuck in the house.

Pause.

So you got home all right last night?

Kevin Sure. No problem.

Sadie I was worried about you.

Kevin *[Smiling]* I wasn't sure if you were going to come tonight.

Sadie Nothing's going to put me off seeing you.

Kevin You mean it, Sadie?

Sadie You know I do.

Kevin Well, no one's going to put me off either.

Sadie Good. All the same, I'd better not be too late tonight.

Kevin No. We don't want to give your father heart failure.

Sadie	*[Laughing]* My father! What was he like last night? I'm sorry about all that, Kevin.
Kevin	Forget it. Parents are all the same.
Sadie	I wonder what you'll be like as a father.
Kevin	Me? I've never really thought about it.
Sadie	Maybe we can't help ending up like our parents. I mean, you're sort of brain-washed from the day you're born.
Kevin	Yeah, a lot of it's subconscious. You don't even know it's happening to you and then one day you end up talking just like them.
Sadie	Frightening, isn't it?
Kevin	You're telling me!
Sadie	You always notice it more in other people. Linda Mullet, she's a classic case ... she's even beginning to look like her mother, and I thought they'd thrown away the mould after she was born!
Kevin	*[Laughing]* It's funny, you and Linda used to be friends.
Sadie	Oh, I don't know, you sort of grow apart, don't you?
Kevin	Yeah, you can say that again. I mean, see our street. I used to love it when I was a kid, but now it drives me up the wall.
Sadie	Same here. Aw, it's great everyone knowing each other, but it gets really claustrophobic everyone knowing your business as well. I mean, if you go into our corner shop, you know, Mrs McConkey's, you don't need to buy a newspaper. That woman's better informed than the BBC ... she knows more about my family than I do!
Kevin	D'you think you'd ever want to leave Belfast?
Sadie	I don't know. Not for good. I'd like to travel though, see what's going on in the rest of the world.
Kevin	I wouldn't mind that myself ... about the furthest I've been is

	Dublin, can you believe it? We've got some cousins down there . . .
Sadie	I wouldn't mind going to America or even China. Somewhere really different, you know.
Kevin	Maybe we should explore the world together . . .
Sadie	Set out on the high seas?
Kevin	Something like that.
Sadie	Only one problem. What do we do for money?
Kevin	Good question.
Sadie	Oh well, no harm in dreaming.
Kevin	You never know Sadie, one of these days.
Sadie	Sure.

She looks at her watch.

Shall we meet here again tomorrow?

Kevin	*[Putting on 'Bogart' accent]* Same place, same time!
Sadie	Half seven.
Kevin	*[Looking at his watch]* Only nineteen hours, twenty-five minutes, and three seconds away!
Sadie	*[To the audience]* We parted before we got to my street. We didn't want to risk meeting my father again.

She exits.

| Kevin | *[To the audience]* I was in a bit of a dream all the way home. You know the sort of thing, on cloud nine, not even looking where I was going . . . all I could think of was meeting Sadie again and both of us wandering along arm in arm by the side of the river. |

*Suddenly, two people, their faces hidden by balaclavas, rush at **Kevin** from either side of the stage. One of them is **Brian**.*

| Brian | All right, McCoy, your numbers up! |

Kevin	Ah! Get off . . . what's going on?
Brian	This is how we deal with traitors . . .

Kevin is beaten up violently. The job done, Brian and his friend run off, leaving Kevin groaning in agony. After a few minutes, Kevin gathers the strength to struggle off the stage.

SCENE 10

A cafe, Belfast city centre, Monday 6 p.m. Sadie enters and places two chairs at a table. She sits with her head in her hands. Brede comes on with two cups of coffee. She sits at the table. She places one of the cups near Sadie, then touches Sadie gently on the arm. Sadie looks up at Brede.

Sadie	Was he badly hurt, Brede?
Brede	A lot of bruises, cuts on his head and leg. He got three stitches in his head.
Sadie	Oh God . . .
Brede	Mr Kelly found him lying unconscious outside the yard late last night. He called an ambulance and Kevin got carted off to hospital.
Sadie	Which hospital is he in?
Brede	They let him out this morning.
Sadie	It happened because of me, didn't it?
Brede	*[Quietly]* Yes, I think so.
Sadie	D'you know who did it?

Brede	There were a couple of them. One of them was Brian Rafferty.
Sadie	I thought he was Kevin's friend.
Brede	It just shows you, doesn't it?
Sadie	Did Kevin ask you to come and tell me?
Brede	He doesn't know I'm here. He's going to meet you tonight as planned. He'll not let you down. But . . . I've come to ask you not to meet him.
Sadie	You want me to let him down?
Brede	It might be best. He's too proud to try and see you again if you don't see him. I know it's hard, but it would be easier if he thought you'd given in.

*Pause. **Sadie** is fighting back her tears.*

Sadie, I'm sorry.

Sadie	I don't know Brede, I don't know . . . I don't know anything at all. I want to see Kevin and he wants to see me and all these people are getting between us . . . Is it right for me to give in to Brian Rafferty and his friends? Is it?
Brede	You don't want Kevin to be hurt again, do you?
Sadie	You know, it's funny . . . people say I'm my own worst enemy . . . I make trouble for myself. They say you should go out with one of your own kind . . . it's easier, less aggravation. Well, for goodness sake, you're all missing the point, aren't you? I'm not going out with Kevin because he's Catholic, or a Mick, or whatever you want to call him . . . I'm going out with him because he's Kevin . . . We like being with each other, we don't want to be with anyone else. I mean, I could have met a Protestant and felt the same way about him as I do about Kevin, but it didn't happen like that, did it? If I meet Kevin, he might get beaten up again; if I don't, he'll hate me . . . What sort of choice is that for anyone? I just want a laugh, I want a bit of fun . . . I just want us to be walking out together, just the two of us, sharing things, spending time together . . . Why can't we do that?

Brede	There's times when it might be all right for a Catholic boy to be walking out with a Protestant girl, but now's not one of them.
Sadie	It's not much to ask to want to walk by the river with someone you like ... I'm not sure. I can't promise, Brede. How can I promise never to see Kevin again? I have to think about it.
Brede	Think carefully, then. There's enough blood, Sadie, without any more getting shed.
	*Brede exits, leaving **Sadie** alone onstage. **Sadie** starts to drink her coffee, then puts it down and pushes the cup away.*
Sadie	*[Almost to herself]* I'm sorry, Kevin. You've got to believe me, I'm really sorry ...
	She rushes off in tears. Music.
	Optional: we see more scenes of Belfast. At first they are all 'tourist'-type pictures – The City Hall, the parks, etc. Then we see a couple of pictures of a street blocked off by soldiers and the RUC.

SCENE 11

By the River Lagan, Monday evening. **Kevin** *enters and sits down stage. His head is bandaged and his arm is in a wrist sling. He is short of breath and finds it an effort to move much. He looks at his watch, then looks around. There is no sign of* **Sadie** *yet.*

Kevin   *[Partly to the audience, partly to himself]* If this is what friends do to you, who needs enemies . . . *[Putting on voice]* Take it easy, Mr McCoy, stay off your work for the next few days. Oh, I'm sure old man Kelly would love that! I'm not the type to sit about the house, it'd be like being in prison. Besides, I want to see Sadie . . . *[Looking at his watch]* She'll get a bit of a fright when she sees me like this . . .

He puts his hand to his head. It's obviously hurting badly.

She's never normally late, I don't understand it . . . Come on, Sadie. Where are you, girl?

He puts his head in his hands and groans.

At this point an elderly gentleman enters. It is **Mr Blake**. *He stands for a few seconds, lighting his pipe, then he notices* **Kevin**. **Kevin** *continues to groan quietly, unaware that he is being watched. He's finding it difficult to keep his head up.* **Mr Blake** *moves towards him, warily at first, then more determined.*

Mr Blake   Excuse me . . . are you all right?

Kevin   Mm?

Mr Blake   You look in a bad way.

Kevin   *[Recovering a bit]* No, I'm fine . . . really . . .

Mr Blake   Have you been here long?

Kevin   I'm all right. I'm waiting on someone . . .

Mr Blake   You don't look all right to me . . . it looks as if there's blood seeping through that bandage . . .

Kevin	It's OK ... I'm fine ... just a bit weak ... had a bit of an accident last night ...
Mr Blake	Should you be out and about so soon? Perhaps I could get you to a doctor, just to check that bandage ... my car's not far away ...

Kevin looks at his watch again.

Kevin	What time do you make it?
Mr Blake	Nearly eight o'clock.
Kevin	Are you sure?
Mr Blake	Is she late then? A woman's prerogative, eh?
Kevin	She's never late.
Mr Blake	Maybe she's not coming.
Kevin	She'll come.
Mr Blake	You sound pretty sure.
Kevin	Well ... I know her.
Mr Blake	I should hope so. *[Smiling]* Nice spot this. I used to come here when I was courting ... a long time ago ... it was one of our favourite meeting places. Elizabeth always loved the river ...
Kevin	Sadie probably got delayed, but she'll be here, I know ...
Mr Blake	Even after we were married, we'd come here of an evening ... Look, son, I'll make a deal with you. You're not looking well at all. I'll walk along the path a bit and then I'll come back, and if your young lady hasn't turned up, I'll give you a lift home, eh?
Kevin	All right.
Mr Blake	Whereabouts d'you live?
Kevin	*[Sighing]* Look, it's very kind of you to offer, but I might as well tell you. I'm a Catholic.
Mr Blake	*[Shrugging his shoulders]* And I might as well tell you, I'm not. But if you think that means I'm going to drop you by the side

of the river, you've got another thing coming. I'll be back in a few minutes, all right?

| Kevin | Sure. |

*As **Mr Blake** starts to walk off, **Sadie** comes rushing on and bumps into him. She recognizes him.*

Sadie	Oh sorry ... Mr Blake? What are you doing here?
Mr Blake	Well, well, Sadie Jackson!
Sadie	*[Seeing Kevin]* Kevin! Oh Kevin, I'm sorry I'm late ...
Kevin	Sadie!
Sadie	What have they done to you?
Kevin	I'm all right, Sadie, it looks worse than it is ... and this gentleman's been looking after me.
Mr Blake	So that's who you were waiting on ... Sadie Jackson ... well, well ... it's a funny old world.
Kevin	You two know each other?
Sadie	Mr Blake was one of my teachers. Haven't seen you for ages, Mr Blake.
Mr Blake	*[Smiling]* Things have been pretty quiet since you left. Now, that young fella of yours looks as if he needs to rest up somewhere and have a good strong cup of tea. I've got my car along the road ... why don't you both come back to my place and join me for some tea?
Sadie	Sounds like a good idea to me, Kevin.
Kevin	OK.
Mr Blake	*[Helping Kevin up]* I'll give my doctor a ring and get him to have a look at your dressings. He's an old friend and I'm sure he'll oblige ...

*They go off. **Sadie** stays behind.*

Sadie	*[To the audience]* Mr Blake was really good. He took us to his house in one of the posher districts of Belfast ... well, posh compared with us. He'd just retired from teaching and he lived in a little bungalow, really nicely done out. He left me and Kevin alone in the lounge while he made the tea.

By now **Kevin** *has re-appeared.*

Kevin	He's all right, isn't he?
Sadie	Aw, he's really nice. We used to call him 'Twinkle Blake' at school because of his eyes. He was one of these teachers everybody liked, always really friendly and open ... Kevin, I'm sorry I was late. You see, Brede came to see me ...
Kevin	Brede? Oh, I see ... she asked you not to come, didn't she?
Sadie	Yes. She was worried about you and I didn't know what to do. But I couldn't bear the thought of you waiting.
Kevin	I'm glad.
Sadie	The thing is, Kevin, I decided I'd come to see you tonight, but I decided it would have to be the last time.
Kevin	Sadie, what are you talking about?
Sadie	It's not because I don't want to see you. You know I do.
Kevin	But you're going to give in to them?
Sadie	It's not a case of giving in.
Kevin	All right, what is it then?
Sadie	I don't want you to get hurt again, that's all.
Kevin	*[Sighing]* I'm sorry, I didn't mean to sound angry with you. It's just that I hate the idea of Brian Rafferty telling me what to do.
Sadie	It's not just Brian Rafferty. If it wasn't him, it would be somebody else. Every time I left you, I'd be wondering if you were going to be beaten up on the way home.
Kevin	We could meet in secret.

Sadie	Yes, but where?
Kevin	Oh, I don't know.
	Mr Blake enters with a tray of tea and biscuits.
Mr Blake	Here we are, some tea, and the doctor's on his way, OK?
Sadie	Thanks.
Mr Blake	You two don't look very happy.
Kevin	We're not.
Mr Blake	Here, have some tea, Kevin. Now do you want to tell me what this is all about?
Sadie	D'you think we're mad, Mr Blake, going out with each other?
Mr Blake	*[Taking a deep breath]* Yes. And I should probably give you good advice and tell you to give it up. But you can't always walk with the crowd, especially if you don't like the way they're walking. I admire you for it. It takes a bit of courage. You were never lacking in that, Sadie.
Sadie	There was a time when I wouldn't go near a Catholic …
Mr Blake	And now here you are going out with one. Sadie, people are just people, and there's good and bad on all sides.
Sadie	But if me going out with Kevin causes so much trouble, is it worth it?
Mr Blake	Only you and Kevin can decide that. If you really like each other, you'll find a way to keep going and, with a bit of luck, in time, everyone will leave you alone. Look, I think you need a few days to recover from all this, both of you. It's not just Kevin's injuries, it's the shock of being attacked.
Sadie	I know, I just can't think straight at the moment.
Kevin	You're not the only one.
Mr Blake	I tell you what, why don't the two of you come round here for supper later in the week?

Sadie	We'd love to, wouldn't we, Kevin?
Kevin	If you don't mind, Mr Blake.
Mr Blake	We'll make it Friday, that'll give you a bit of time to rest and get your strength back . . . and no one will bother you out here. OK?
Kevin	Sure.
Mr Blake	All right, I'll clear this away.
	Mr Blake takes the tray and the mugs and exits.
Sadie	Well, Kevin, I'll see you on Friday then?
Kevin	Yeah.
	They smile.
	Sadie, don't you worry, I'll be OK.
Sadie	You take it easy, all right? I want you fit and well for Friday.
	Kevin goes off.

● ●

SCENE 12

Sadie's street.

Sadie	*[To the audience]* It was hard not seeing Kevin until Friday. I was wondering what he was getting up to. I couldn't phone him or anything. I just had to be patient. Was he seeing Kate Kelly? She always used to fancy him. After all, it would be a lot easier for him to go out with one of his own kind.
	Police and fire engine sirens. Tommy comes running on.
Tommy	Sadie! Have you seen what's going on outside?
Sadie	What are you talking about?
Tommy	It's Mrs McConkey's shop. It's on fire!
	Sadie and Tommy run to another part of the acting area and stand watching the fire (perhaps from behind the barrier). We hear

the sound of people shouting, sirens etc. **Mr and Mrs Jackson, Mr and Mrs Mullet, Linda Mullet,** *and other neighbours, come on and stand in groups, staring at the fire.*

Mrs Jackson	God help us all, it could be our turn next.
Mrs Mullet	And to think I was only in there a few hours ago …
Mr Mullet	Don't you worry, whoever was behind this will soon pay for it.
Mr Jackson	Oh yeah, if they ever find them.
Mrs Mullet	It's funny, there was a young girl in there when I was in. She wasn't from round here.
Mr Jackson	You think she had something to do with it?
Mrs Mullet	Well, you never know, do you?
Sadie	Tommy, I don't believe this. We've been going in there for years and look at it, just a mass of flames.
Tommy	They say it was a petrol bomb …
Sadie	Well, Mrs McConkey's shop's a goner for sure …
Tommy	Let's hope she's not …
Sadie	You mean she was in there?
Tommy	Oh yeah, she was in the back shop doing her stock-taking …
Sadie	Oh my God …
Tommy	They've taken her to hospital. God knows how they got her out.
Mr Jackson	There's not much we can do here.
Mrs Jackson	I think we need a good strong cup of tea after all this.
Mr Mullet	Nice of you to offer …

Mrs Jackson frowns. She hadn't meant to invite the Mullets. They all go off except Linda. Linda joins Sadie and Tommy at the barrier.

Linda	Hello, Sadie, Tommy …

Sadie	Oh hi, Linda. I might have known you'd be here. Never miss a show, eh?
Linda	And I'm surprised you're not out with your Mick boyfriend tonight.
Sadie	It's none of your business.
Linda	Maybe it is my business ...
Tommy	Look, Linda, just drop it, right?
Linda	Maybe there's more to this than meets the eye.
Sadie	What are you talking about?
Linda	Call it coincidence, call it what you like ... When my mother was in there earlier having a blether with Mrs McConkey, there was a girl in there, a stranger, looking for you, Sadie ...
Tommy	Sadie, what's she talking about?
Sadie	I've no idea.
Linda	Oh yes, you have. 'Cause you know as well as I do who that stranger was ... it was Kevin McCoy's sister, Brede.
Tommy	Well, what's Brede got to do with this?
Linda	You never know. You don't get many Catholics coming round here, do you?
Sadie	Are you suggesting that Brede might have put a bomb in Mrs McConkey's shop?
Linda	Not exactly, but she could have been sent to spy out the lie of the land.
Tommy	Linda, don't be stupid. Brede wouldn't have anything to do with this. You know something, Linda? You're just like your mother, you talk a lot of rubbish!
	*Tommy goes off, followed by **Linda**.*
Linda	[*Going*] Tommy, I never thought I'd hear you talking to me like that ... Tommy, all I meant was ...

Sadie	To be honest, Linda, I don't know what Tommy sees in you! *[To the audience]* Mrs McConkey died. We all knew she had been badly injured ... but ... well, it was terrible seeing it on a newspaper stand the next morning ... 'SHOP BURNED DOWN. WOMAN DEAD'. It was so anonymous, so cold, so detached from reality ... it wasn't just any old shop, it wasn't just a woman ... it was Mrs McConkey ... we used to make fun of her, call her names ...

*Sadie moves away from the barrier and sits on one of the chairs, still shocked by the news of **Mrs McConkey's** death.*

● ●

SCENE 13

Mr Blake's house. Sadie is still onstage from the previous scene. Mr Blake comes on and gives her a cup of tea.

Mr Blake	Here, Sadie, drink this.
Sadie	It's been quite a day, Mr Blake.
Mr Blake	I know.
Sadie	I'm sorry for landing on your doorstep like this, but I didn't know where else to go.
Mr Blake	Shouldn't you be at work?
Sadie	Oh, I've been there all right, for the last time. Some of the girls had seen me with Kevin and it got back to the supervisor ... she's a right old bitch, so today she started asking all sorts of questions, being really nasty about Kevin ... I told her to get lost, I told her to mind her own business. So that was that, I lost my job. Now I don't know what I'm going to do.
Mr Blake	I tell you what, until you get something better you can work for me.
Sadie	For you?
Mr Blake	Yes, I could do with a bit of help around here, cleaning and cooking. It'd only be part-time, but it would help me out and maybe help you out as well.

Sadie	Are you serious, Mr Blake?
Mr Blake	*[Going off]* The job's yours if you want it.
Sadie	Wait till I tell my mother I've lost one job and got another all in the same day . . .
	*Mr Blake has now left the stage. **Kevin** enters.*
Kevin	*[To the audience]* I fell into the habit of meeting Sadie at Mr Blake's. Sometimes we'd spend the afternoon sitting in the garden, all three of us, chatting. Other times, Sadie and I would find ourselves going off for long walks . . .
Sadie	*[To the audience]* These were the good times . . .

● ●

SCENE 14

	*A park near **Mr Blake's** house. **Kevin** and **Sadie** walk down towards the front of the acting area.*
Kevin	It's nice being able to walk about without having to look over our shoulders all the time.
Sadie	Well, no one knows us round here.
Kevin	Back home I feel I'm being followed all the time . . .
Sadie	Well, at least you don't need to worry about that here.
	*Kate Kelly appears upstage. She watches **Kevin** and **Sadie**.*
Kevin	I'd better be going now . . . I'll see you tomorrow.
Sadie	Yeah. I'd better be getting home as well. See you tomorrow?
Kevin	*[Smiling]* What do you think?
	*Kevin and Sadie embrace and part. **Kevin** smiles.*
Sadie	*[Going]* See you!
	*Sadie goes off. **Kevin** turns to go off in the opposite direction and meets **Kate**.*
Kate	Long time no see, Kevin.

Kevin	Kate!
Kate	You're so mysterious these days. I mean, what do you do with yourself all day? You don't seem to have time for your old friends these days.
Kevin	Some of them are no longer my friends. I don't particularly like getting beaten up.
Kate	It wouldn't be friends who did that.
Kevin	Kate, I know who did it.
Kate	You're thinking of Brian Rafferty, aren't you? He says you've been going around slandering him. He's not pleased.
Kevin	I don't care if he's pleased or not. You keep out of it, Kate. Now, if you don't mind, I'd like to get home.
Kate	Just a minute, Kevin. I want to know something.
Kevin	What?
Kate	Is it all over with us?
Kevin	Kate . . . it's not as if we were going steady or anything.
Kate	I thought we were.
Kevin	Well, I didn't.
Kate	Who is she?
Kevin	Look, Kate, you've got it all wrong . . .
Kate	Oh, have I?
Kevin	We were just friends. I thought you understood that . . .
Kate	Oh, I understand all right, Kevin.
Kevin	Good.
Kate	You're cruel and horrible, Kevin McCoy, and I hate you! *[Screaming]* I hate you!

Kate runs off. Kevin looks confused and slightly stunned. He sits down and puts his head in his hands. Music.

SCENE 15

Kevin's *street.* Kevin *remains sitting with his head in his hands.* Sadie *appears on the other side of the acting area.*

Sadie   *[To the audience]* It wasn't easy going out with Kevin ... I mean, we got on well and everything ... oh sure, we had arguments from time to time, I'm not denying it, but it was all the other pressures that made it difficult ... My parents wanting to know where I was all the time, the gossiping tongues, people that used to be my friends, the threats ... oh yes, I got them too ... sometimes I couldn't sleep at nights for thinking about it ...

We hear Sadie *dreaming. The voices are distorted, maybe with an echo effect.* Sadie *closes her eyes, trying to shut out the voices. (This scene could be done as a dream sequence using voice-overs on tape, or it could be done 'live' with* Linda, Steve, *and later on* Brede *and* Brian *actually onstage saying their lines.)*

Linda   *[Off]* Not out with your Mick boyfriend the night, Sadie?

Sadie   *[Off]* I've nothing to talk to you about, Linda Mullet.

Linda   *[Off]* You needn't pretend you don't know who I'm talking about.

Steve   *[Off]* Will you be marching on the Twelfth, Sadie?

Linda   *[Off]* Her Mick boyfriend won't let her.

Sadie   *[Off]* Just leave me alone!

Steve   *[Off]* Course, her brother's not much better ... won't even join the Lodge ...

Sadie   *[Off]* Leave Tommy out of it ... Just leave us alone!

Sadie   *[To the audience]* I wasn't the only one having trouble sleeping. Kevin didn't tell me at first but he was having nightmares as well ... and sometimes the dreams became reality ...

Sadie *exits.*

Brede	*[Off]* Have you been upsetting Kate again?
Kevin	*[Off]* She upset herself.
Brede	*[Off]* Kate Kelly can cause trouble ... she's been hanging around with Brian Rafferty a lot ...
Kevin	*[Off]* Maybe they'll be good for each other ...
Brian	*[Off]* Kevin! There was a time when you were ready to fight for one Ireland ...
	There's no other way, Kevin! No other way! There's times you have to stand up and be counted!

*Suddenly the music and effects stop and two British **soldiers** burst on to the stage. One of them grabs **Kevin** and hauls him to his feet.*

Soldier 1	All right, on your feet, sonny!
Kevin	What the hell's going on?
Soldier 2	Kevin McCoy?
Kevin	Eh?
Soldier 1	That's him all right.
Kevin	Look, what do you want?
Soldier 2	We've got something to show you ... I think it's something you lost.
Kevin	I don't know what you're talking about ...

*One of the **soldiers** holds up a rifle covered with a blanket.*

Soldier 2	Guess what we've got in here ...
Kevin	Eh?
Soldier 1	Oh, little Mick's playing dumb ... playing little games with us. Oh, well, want to see what we've got?
Kevin	Do what you like, it's got nothing to do with me!
Soldier 2	I think it might, son.

*The **soldier** takes off the blanket and holds the rifle in front of **Kevin**.*

Surprise, surprise! Looks familiar, eh?

Kevin	What's that got to do with me?
Soldier 1	So you're saying it's not yours?
Kevin	What would I want with a rifle?
Soldier 2	Oh, I couldn't possibly imagine. *[Grabbing him]* All right, if it's not yours, whose is it?
Kevin	*[Shouting]* I don't know.
Soldier 1	Well it was found at Kelly's Scrapyard, where you work.
Kevin	Hard luck, I've been off work for the past week. Now, if you don't mind, I'd like to go home.
Soldier 1	You're a bit of a comedian, aren't you? Come on, let's get him down to the barracks ...
Kevin	Leave off ... I've done nothing wrong I'm telling you ...

*They drag him off the stage. **Brede** comes on.*

Brede	*[To the audience]* They questioned my brother all through the night. I went to the barracks and told them about Kate Kelly and how she had a grudge against Kevin. Kate's evidence against Kevin was pretty weak anyway. She thought she saw Kevin hiding the rifle in the yard. But Kate wasn't the real culprit, it was Brian Rafferty. They say revenge is sweet ...

***Kevin** re-appears. **Brede** looks at him sympathetically, he returns her look, then walks past her to **Sadie** who has now appeared at the other side of the acting area.*

Kevin	I waited in the alley for him this morning, Sadie. I was like a killer stalking my victim. I got him all right. I let him have it ... it was as if the devil was in me ... I just kept on hitting him ...
Sadie	You didn't kill him, did you?
Kevin	No, but I could have.

Brede exits.

Kevin	Do you think I was wrong to go after him?
Sadie	I don't know what good it does. But it's what you think that counts.
Kevin	I don't know what I think. I felt sick when I stood and looked down at him. It's not that I care very much about Brian. I wanted to fight him, but after I'd got him down there lying at my feet, I wished I hadn't done it. I'd sunk to his level. It was as if I'd been stained by the very thing that's been making me sick . . . All this meaningless revenge . . . what good does it do? I mean, what's next on the agenda? More blood?

Pause.

[To the audience] Sadie and I spent a lot of time at Mr Blake's. Sometimes all three of us would get in his car and go for a run in the country. We'd take a picnic, make a day of it . . .

Music.

● ●

SCENE 16

In the country. **Mr Blake** *and* **Sadie** *are lying on a blanket. They take some food out of a picnic hamper.* **Kevin** *sits beside them. Conversation is in full flow. Music fades.*

Sadie	My mum's that worried about me. She's been trying to fix me up with a job . . .
Mr Blake	Well, it shows how much she cares, Sadie.

Sadie	It's the butcher round the corner. They were wanting someone on the cash desk. Can you imagine me sitting in a butcher's shop all day long?
Mr Blake	Well, at least it's a job, Sadie.
Sadie	Not for me.
Kevin	So how did you get out of it?
Sadie	Well, I went in to see the manager, just to please my mother, you know ... and I told him I was a vegetarian and the sight of blood makes me boke!
	They all burst out laughing.
	He said that under the circumstances it might not be the best job for me!
Kevin	Trust you, Sadie!
Mr Blake	Ah, it's nice to hear you two laughing. Whatever happens we mustn't forget how to laugh.
Kevin	I bet your mother was furious.
Sadie	She was raging. She's not been into the butcher's for days.
Mr Blake	Aw well ...
Sadie and Kevin	*[Together, slightly sending Mr Blake up]* I suppose we'd better be getting home, after all it is getting late ...
	Mr Blake laughs and they gather up the picnic and start towards the car.
Sadie	Thanks for bringing us.
Mr Blake	It's my pleasure, we must come again ...
	Suddenly they freeze as we hear the following news report ...
Newsreader	*[Off]* BBC Radio Ulster News at six o'clock. Police are tonight investigating an accident on the Antrim road in which a retired Belfast school teacher and his two passengers were injured when their car left the road. Police suspect that the wheels of

the car were deliberately loosened, causing the car to veer out of control . . .

Mr Blake exits.

Sadie   *[To the audience]* After the crash, we decided not to go on meeting at Mr Blake's. It was too dangerous. I went on working for him, cooking and cleaning and waiting for Kevin to phone to arrange our next meeting . . .

Kevin   *[To the audience]* I had decided not to phone.

He goes off.

• •

SCENE 17

*Sadie's house, the twelfth day of July. We can hear the bands playing and marching outside. **Sadie** is sitting trying to write a letter to **Kevin**.*

Sadie   *[To herself]* Dear Kevin, today's the Twelfth, almost three weeks since I last saw you. The Orange bands are driving me mad, just like they used to drive you mad . . .

*She crumples up the letter. **Tommy** comes in quietly.*

Tommy   Sadie? Sadie, is there anything wrong?

66

Sadie	No, Tommy. Everything's fine, just fine.
Tommy	I'm going to watch the parade, would you like to come?
Sadie	That's the last thing I want to do.
Tommy	Dad was on at me again this morning about joining the Lodge.
Sadie	Are you going to? That's it, Tommy, join up and be a good Orangeman and make everybody happy . . . They might even give you a bowler hat, if you're lucky.
Tommy	I said no.
Sadie	Good on you, Tommy. I thought we'd lost you.
Tommy	There's no harm in watching the parade though. It keeps Dad happy . . . at least he thinks I'm showing a bit of interest.
Sadie	Well, I'm going to get as far away from here as possible. I'm going to Bangor.
Tommy	Who with?
Sadie	Don't worry, I haven't seen Kevin for weeks.
	Tommy walks off.

● ●

SCENE 18

	Bangor. Music in the background. **Kevin** *comes on from the opposite side of the acting area to* **Sadie**.
Kevin	*[To the audience]* I went to Bangor for the day . . . you see, the year I met Sadie we'd spent the Twelfth there . . .
Sadie	I thought I might bump into you . . .
	They smile and move towards each other.
Kevin	*[To the audience]* We started seeing one another again . . .
Sadie	*[To the audience]* We went back to meeting at Mr Blake's . . .
Kevin	*[To the audience]* We tried to be careful . . .

Sadie	*[To the audience]* For a while we thought we were going to get away with it . . .
Kevin	We should have known better . . .

*Kevin walks slowly off. As he does so, **Tommy** comes back on.*

● ●

SCENE 19

*Sadie's room. **Sadie** stands in the same position as in the scene before. She is very still. **Tommy** moves towards her.*

Tommy	Sadie, I've got some bad news . . . Mr Blake's neighbour phoned . . .
Sadie	You mean Moira? . . . Tommy . . . what's happened?
Tommy	It's Mr Blake . . . he's dead.
Sadie	No!

He puts his arms round her. She doesn't move.

Tommy	Someone threw a petrol bomb into his house last night. The place went up in minutes and he didn't have a chance . . . I'm sorry, Sadie . . . I'm sorry . . .
Sadie	*[In tears]* Oh God . . . it's my fault, Tommy . . . it's all my fault . . .
Tommy	You mustn't say that . . .
Sadie	It's true . . .

*Sadie moves away from **Tommy**.*

Sadie	I shouldn't have let him get involved, we shouldn't have spent so much time at his house . . . Remember when we were at school? People used to make fun of Mr Blake . . . they liked him, but they gave him a hard time. He always took it in good spirits, he was never one to hold a grudge . . . he was nice, wasn't he? Too nice for his own good maybe . . . if it hadn't been for him, Kevin and I would have split up long ago . . . I once asked him why he

was helping Kevin and me . . . he said that we deserved a chance, he said that we had a right to be together . . . he gave us hope . . .

*During the speech, **Tommy** exits and, by the end of it, **Kevin** has come on and stands beside **Sadie**. As **Tommy** and **Kevin** pass one another, they exchange a glance. **Kevin** has a suitcase with him . . . we are now at Belfast docks.*

SCENE 20

*Belfast docks, midday. **Kevin** is standing by **Sadie**, holding his suitcase.*

Kevin   I've had enough, Sadie. I never thought I'd see the day when I'd want to leave Belfast . . . But I'm sick of it all . . . sick of all the killings. I keep wondering who put that bomb through Mr Blake's window. Was it one of my so-called friends? Would Brian Rafferty really go that far?

Sadie   It could have been someone I know, someone from my street.

Kevin   What sort of place has this become? I'd like to walk down a street where there were no soldiers with guns, no policemen with their fingers on triggers . . . and no bloody graffiti on the walls . . . there must be more to life than all of that . . .

Sadie   My mother was shouting at me again yesterday. Everything's back to normal. It's nearly a week now since they buried Mr Blake . . . 'Well Sadie, you've learned your lesson now' . . . that's what she said, no kiddin', and she meant it. My father is convinced it was one of your lot . . . I told him just to go to hell. I said it could just as easily have been him next door, your good friend Mr Mullet . . . I thought he was going to hit me . . . he stood up and came over to me and looked me in the eye . . . but before he could say anything, I started crying, I felt I was going to burst . . . so he didn't hit me, he put his arms round me and held me. That was worse - he was trying to comfort me and I just felt cold all through my body ... I wish to God he had hit me, it would have made it easier!

Kevin   Parents! My mother thinks I should have taken back my old job at Kelly's. She doesn't want to face up to things ... I can understand it in a way, they've got to go on living in that street. Brede was all right though, she helped me pack ... she understands, she knows ... I'll miss Brede, you know, I really will ... I'll miss Belfast ... *[Laughing]* I'm feeling homesick already and I'm not even on the ferry ...

Sadie   Did you think I wouldn't come?

Kevin   I knew you'd be here ... the only trouble is, I don't want to say goodbye to you ...

Sadie   Kevin, I haven't come to say goodbye ...

Kevin   *[Laughing nervously]* No, of course, we'll see each other again.

Sadie   You don't understand, do you? Look, I've bought a ticket. I'm coming with you. That is, if you don't mind?

Kevin   Sadie, are you kidding?

Sadie   *[Excited]* I've no luggage. I couldn't walk out of the house with a case, so you'll have to take me as I stand.

Kevin   Sadie, this is the best news I've had in months.

He picks her up and swings her round. They kiss.

Sadie   *[Smiling]* Come on then, let's get aboard. What are we waiting for?

Kevin   Nothing. London here we come!

Kevin picks up his case and they turn to go, but freeze. We hear their voices on tape again, with music in the background.

Sadie   *[Off]* And that was just the beginning ...

Kevin   *[Off]* You should have seen Sadie on the boat. I've never seen anyone looking so ill in all my life, honestly ...

Sadie	*[Laughing]* Ssh ... shut up, Kevin ... you're not meant to tell them about that ...

We hear them both laughing, then the laughter fades.

Newsreader	*[Off]* Capital Radio, Newsflash. A bomb has exploded in the centre of London today. It is understood that the explosion was caused by a car bomb. Unconfirmed reports say that at least five people have been killed and over a hundred have been injured. No one has claimed responsibility for the incident but a police spokesman confirmed that eight people have been detained under the Prevention of Terrorism Act. An emergency telephone number has been given for relatives and friends. The number is 01-779 ... *[fade]*.

As the newsflash fades, the music comes up.

*During the newsflash, **Sadie** and **Kevin** turn back to face the audience. The other members of the cast come back onto the stage. They all stand motionless as they hear the news report.*

After the newsflash, the music builds, then fades.

Activities

Year 7

KEY STAGE 3 FRAMEWORK OBJECTIVES	RELEVANT ACTIVITIES CHAPTER(S)
Sentence level	
4 Tense management	Conflict in Ireland
8 Starting paragraphs	Conflict in Ireland
9 Main point of paragraph	Conflict in Ireland
12 Sequencing paragraphs	Conflict in Ireland
13a) Information	Conflict in Ireland
13b) Recount	Conflict in Ireland
13c) Explanation	Conflict in Ireland
Reading	
1 Locate information	Conflict in Ireland
2 Extract information	Conflict in Ireland; Writing a Newspaper Article; Mixed Marriages
4 Note-making	Conflict in Ireland
5 Evaluate sources	Conflict in Ireland
6 Active reading	Opposites or Parallels?; Violence; Different Viewpoints
7 Identify main ideas	Opposites or Parallels?; Violence
8 Infer and deduce	Violence
9 Distinguish writer's views	Opposites or Parallels?; Violence; Different Viewpoints
16 Author attitudes	Opposites or Parallels?; Different Viewpoints
18 Response to a play	Violence
Writing	
1 Drafting process	Conflict in Ireland; Writing a Newspaper Article
2 Planning formats	Conflict in Ireland; Opposites or Parallels?
6 Characterisation	Different Viewpoints; Mixed Marriages
10 Organize texts appropriately	Conflict in Ireland; Writing a Newspaper Article
11 Present information	Conflict in Ireland; Writing a Newspaper Article
12 Develop logic	Conflict in Ireland; Writing a Newspaper Article
14 Evocative description	Writing a Newspaper Article
15 Express a view	Opposites or Parallels?
Speaking and listening	
1 Clarify through talk	Opposites or Parallels?; Unscripted Drama
3 Shape a presentation	Conflict in Ireland
4 Answers, instructions, explanations	Conflict in Ireland; Opposites or Parallels?
5 Put a point of view	Opposites or Parallels?
6 Recall main points	Opposites or Parallels?; Violence
7 Pertinent questions	Conflict in Ireland; Opposites or Parallels?; Violence
11 Range of roles	Opposites or Parallels?
12 Exploratory talk	Opposites or Parallels?; Unscripted Drama
13 Collaboration	Conflict in Ireland; Opposites or Parallels?; Unscripted Drama
14 Modify views	Conflict in Ireland; Opposites or Parallels?; Unscripted Drama
15 Explore in role	Violence; Different Viewpoints; Unscripted Drama
16 Collaborate on scripts	Violence; Different Viewpoints; Unscripted Drama
19 Evaluate presentations	Conflict in Ireland; Opposites or Parallels?; Unscripted Drama

Year 8

Key Stage 3 Framework Objectives	Relevant Activities Chapter(s)
Sentence level	
7 Cohesion and coherence	Conflict in Ireland
8 Subject-specific conventions	Conflict in Ireland
Reading	
1 Combine information	Conflict in Ireland
2 Independent research	Conflict in Ireland
3 Note-making formats	Conflict in Ireland
5 Trace developments	Opposites or Parallels?; Violence; Mixed Marriages
6 Bias and objectivity	Conflict in Ireland; Different Viewpoints
7 Implied and explicit meanings	Violence
10 Development of key ideas	Opposites or Parallels?; Violence
16 Cultural context	Opposites or Parallels?; Violence; Different Viewpoints
Writing	
1 Effective planning	Conflict in Ireland; Writing a Newspaper Article
2 Anticipate reader reaction	Conflict in Ireland; Writing a Newspaper Article
10 Effective information	Conflict in Ireland; Writing a Newspaper Article
11 Explain complex ideas	Conflict in Ireland
12 Formal description	Conflict in Ireland; Writing a Newspaper Article
13 Present a case persuasively	Opposites or Parallels?
14 Develop an argument	Opposites or Parallels?
16 Balanced analysis	Conflict in Ireland
17 Integrate evidence	Conflict in Ireland
Speaking and listening	
1 Evaluate own speaking	Conflict in Ireland
2 Develop recount	Violence
3 Formal presentation	Conflict in Ireland; Opposites or Parallels?
5 Questions to clarify or refine	Opposites or Parallels?
7 Listen for a specific purpose	Opposites or Parallels?; Violence
10 Hypothesis and speculation	Unscripted Drama
11 Building on others	Conflict in Ireland; Opposites or Parallels?; Unscripted Drama
12 Varied roles in discussion	Conflict in Ireland; Opposites or Parallels?
14 Dramatic techniques	Violence; Different Viewpoints; Unscripted Drama
15 Work in role	Violence; Different Viewpoints; Unscripted Drama
16 Collaborative presentation	Violence; Different Viewpoints; Unscripted Drama

Conflict in Ireland

For this activity, you will need to do some research, some writing, and a short presentation about conflict in Ireland. (You may wish to work in pairs or small groups, focusing in detail on one or two different topics/events, or you could look at the overall history, giving just an outline of each topic or event.)

RESEARCH

1 Copy out the grid below, leaving plenty of space in each box for you to make notes. The headings in the grid show key events and topics in Ireland's history.

Event/Topic	Notes
The plantation of Ulster, 1610	
Battle of the Boyne, 1690	
William of Orange ('King Billy')	
12th July and the Orange order	
Catholics/Republicans	
Protestants/Unionists	
Ireland divided, 1921	
Civil rights, 1960s	
British troops sent into Northern Ireland, 1969	
IRA (Irish Republican Army)	
Anglo-Irish Agreement, 1985	
Good Friday Agreement, 1998	

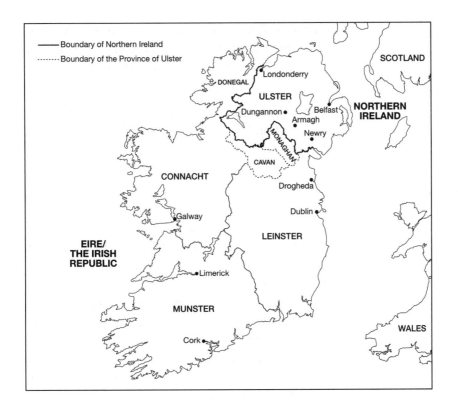

Boundary of Northern Ireland
Boundary of the Province of Ulster

2   Do some research on each topic (or a selected few), using whatever sources you can find, e.g. books, magazines, newspapers, the Internet, people who have views on the conflict. Some web sites that you might find useful are:
www.bbc.co.uk/history
www.cain.ulst.ac.uk/events/peace
www.schoolshistory.org.uk

When you are researching, use the skills you have been taught to gather relevant information, e.g.:

- skimming text (to gain an overall picture of the information and ideas)
- scanning text (to pick out key words, facts, and features)
- use indexes and glossaries
- use menus on screen to pick out the most important features
- use links to other web sites.

Remember to note the sources of your information and think about how reliable they are. Don't forget that people's memories are not always accurate and their opinions can be biased!

3   Think about how you record your information. You may wish to use diagrams, maps and flow charts. The outline map and grid (see pages 76 and 77) are just starting points.

• •

WRITING

1   When you have finished your research, write a short report for your class. Decide on the best way to present the information you have found, then write a first draft. Think about:
● the main heading and sub-headings
● visuals, such as maps, diagrams, flow–charts, photographs, etc.
● the use of facts and figures
● the use of the present tense and third person (Remember that this is a factual text, so should not contain your personal opinions.)
● a clear explanation of words that your reader may not be familiar with
● the use of bullets for listed information
● how you lead your reader through your report – make sure there is a logical sequence to your ideas
● the use of paragraphs and topic sentences (sentences at the start of paragraphs, which indicate what the rest of the paragraph is about).

2   When you have finished your first draft, swap it with a partner, or another pair or group. Review each other's work, pointing out the best features and suggesting areas that could be developed further.

3   With the feedback, work on a final draft of your report. Don't forget to proof-read it for spelling and punctuation errors!

PRESENTATION

Give a short talk or presentation about the work you have done. This could be alone, with a partner, or in a group.

1 Prepare the talk carefully. Think about:
   - what visuals, if any, you would like to display
   - the structure of your talk
   - whether you need some notes to refer to while speaking
   - what sort of questions people might ask, and how you might answer them.

2 Rehearse your talk with others, checking that it is clearly sequenced so that your audience can follow what you are saying.

3 After your presentation, think about what aspects went well and what you might be able to improve on next time you do a presentation.

ACTIVITIES

ACROSS THE BARRICADES

Opposites or parallels?

This is what the author, Joan Lingard, says about her series of books about Kevin and Sadie.

> 'My aim was to make [the books] as balanced as possible. I did not want to be on one side or the other. I wanted to be for the Protestants and for the Catholics, seeing the good and the bad points in both. I wanted to write in a way that would make my readers think about prejudice and the way we tend to divide up society into 'us' and 'them'.'

In *The Twelfth of July*, the prequel to *Across the Barricades*, Joan Lingard alternates the chapters, moving between the Protestant and Catholic communities, so that they each fill a similar space in the book. There are many ways in which the two sides are balanced in *Across the Barricades*, too.

1   Think about the parallels which run through the story of *Across the Barricades*. Draw up list of similarities between Sadie and Kevin. Think about:
- their parents (and their relationship with them)
- their siblings (and their relationship with them)
- where they live
- the type of houses they live in
- their jobs
- their friends
- their personalities (strengths and weaknesses)
- their views on violence.

2   Now draw up a list of the differences between Kevin and Sadie. Think about:
- their age and gender
- their religion

- their political views.

3   On balance, do you think the differences outweigh the similarities or vice versa? Write a short persuasive text, giving your viewpoint. Try to persuade your reader to share it.

Remember that when you write a persuasive text, you can give emphasis to your views by using repetition, exaggeration, and rhetorical questions. Try to anticipate arguments from people who hold different views – for example, how would you counter the argument that people's backgrounds will always influence them, and that Kevin and Sadie can never escape their backgrounds?

4   Hold a debate on the issue. The topic could be 'The differences between Sadie Jackson and Kevin McCoy outweigh the similarities'. Follow these steps to conduct an effective debate:

Step 1
Each side discusses the issue in their group and lists points to be made.

Step 2
Each side appoints a main speaker.

Step 3
An impartial chair person (possibly your teacher) is appointed.

Step 4
The main speakers present their cases.

Step 5
The 'floor' is opened for discussion, so that everyone who wishes to speak or ask questions can do so.

Step 6
A vote is taken on the issue.

Remember, it is important to listen carefully to everyone's contributions and to try and respond to them, rather than just putting forward your own viewpoint.

Violence

Violence is one of the main themes in *Across the Barricades*. The story is set during the Troubles in Northern Ireland in the early 1970s, when the violence affected the whole community: civilians, military, and paramilitary groups.

How does the author use violence to:
- structure the plot
- reveal more about the characters
- affect the reader's emotions and views?

VIOLENCE IN THE PLOT STRUCTURE

The author often uses a violent incident to create a turning point in the story structure. How do the following incidents change the course of the story?

1   When Brede is seriously injured during a street fight, and has to go to hospital. What effect does this have on key characters and their relationship?

2   When Mr Blake is killed by a petrol bomb, how do Kevin and Sadie react? What decision does it trigger?

HOW CHARACTERS REACT TO VIOLENCE

Violence affects people in different ways at different times. What do we learn about characters during the following violent incidents?

1   In a dream-like sequence, Kevin and Sadie remember the street fighting in their gangs. How does the author convey the excitement and thrill of violence, then the horror?

2   Kevin is beaten up by his 'friend' Brian Rafferty and his gang. What effect does this have on Kevin? What does he feel and how does he decide to react?

3   When a petrol bomb kills Mrs McConkey, how do different characters react, e.g. Mr Mullet, Mrs Mullet, Linda? What do their reactions tell us about them?

4   At the end of Scene 15, Kevin attacks Brian. How does it make him feel? Does he regret it or does it make him feel better?

• •

THE READER'S EMOTIONS AND VIEW

1   The reader is kept aware of the on-going violence in the setting because the playscript is interspersed with new bulletins, describing shootings, bombs, and riots. (For example, Scene 1, the bulletin about a petrol bomb in Falls Road; Scene 6, the shooting in West Belfast.) Think about:
   ● how these bulletins create an atmosphere of on-going violence and danger
   ● why weather reports are often tacked onto the end of the bulletins
   ● whether or not it matters that the reader doesn't know the people involved in these incidents
   ● what the final bulletin (at the very end of the playscript) tells us about the violence – have Sadie and Kevin escaped it by going to London?

2   In pairs or small groups, act out one of these violent scenes. Think carefully about what your character feels, and how you can convey these feelings through expression and body language, as well as through what the character says and does. Give a short performance in front of the class.

3   After the performance, stay in role, but imagine you are phoning a good friend. Describe what has just happened and how you feel. Another student could take on the role of a sympathetic friend, and listen carefully to what is being said. He or she should make comments and ask questions, helping to clarify what has happened and speculate on what the effects might be.

ACTIVITIES

ACROSS THE BARRICADES

Different viewpoints

1 Read the following quotations. They are all taken from the playscript and are spoken by Mr Blake, Brian Rafferty or Mr Jackson.

Your task is to decide who says what. However, do not look up the speeches in your playscript. Instead, think about the ideas and attitudes being expressed, and which character is most likely to say them, and to whom. (Before you start on this task, you may want to jot down a few notes about what you know about these three characters already.) Work with a partner, so you can discuss your ideas.

All I want to know, Kevin, is one thing, are you a good patriot? ... You believe in the cause, don't you ... We have to be prepared to fight for what we believe in, don't we. I mean you are ready to fight?

Ah it's nice to hear you two laughing. Whatever happens we mustn't forget how to laugh.

You've missed all the action. Doyle's Bar got hit by the Prods. But don't worry, they're going to pay for this. They'd burn us out to the last man if we let them.

You two go home, I've got some unfinished business with this Mick.

You don't seem to realize that we're a family and what you do affects us all ... next time you choose to go for a walk, you go for a walk with one of your own kind!

That's not the way you once talked. There was a time when you were full of fighting to get the six counties back from the English. A united Ireland! Up the rebels! What's happened to all that?

People are just people, and there's good and bad on all sides.

I always go to the Lodge on a Tuesday.

You can't always walk with the crowd, especially if you don't like the way they're walking. I admire you for it. It takes a bit of courage. You were never lacking in that, Sadie.

2   Write a short extract of playscript. Imagine that Brian Rafferty and Mr Jackson hear that Kevin and Sadie are leaving Belfast and rush down to the docks. They arrive just in time to see the ferry leaving. Then they see each other. Think about:
- what they feel
- what they say
- how they look
- whether they get drawn into a physical conflict
- what makes them part
- stage directions.

3   Act out your short scene. Invite comments and suggestions for improvement from your audience.

Unscripted drama

1   As a group, choose one of the following scenes to improvise:

1) One evening, Sadie and Kevin are sitting in the kitchen, having a snack, when Mr and Mrs Jackson return unexpectedly. Linda and Tommy also arrive (Linda has given Mr Jackson the tip off that Sadie and Kevin have spent the day together.)

2) Sadie and Kevin, both sets of parents, and Tommy and Brede, all meet at the docks. The Jacksons and McCoys try to persuade Sadie and Kevin not to leave. Tommy and Brede try to keep the peace between the families.

2   In preparation for your improvisation, follow the steps below.

Step 1

Decide who will play which role.

Step 2

Jot down four adjectives that you think describe your character.

Step 3

Think about how you can relay these aspects of your character through tone of voice, body language, facial expression, and gesture.

Step 4

Consider how your character would interact with the others. Note that there will be differences depending on who you are talking to, e.g. Sadie may be defiant towards her parents, but conciliatory towards Tommy.

Step 5

Decide on any props that you may need for the scene, e.g. a suitcase, tickets, a table and chairs.

Step 6

As a group, discuss what the general outcome of the scene will be, but do not script it.

3   Perform your scene in front of the class, or another group. Ask your audience to identify who is playing which role.

4   After your performance, evaluate your presentation. Think about:
    ● its strengths
    ● how it might be improved
    ● whether you feel you understand your character and their relationships with others better as a result of this role playing.

Writing a Newspaper Article

Read the extract from the novel, below.

They took the road that ran close round by the coast, winding and twisting beside the sea. The water looked green today, tipped with white.

Mr Blake exclaimed suddenly.

'What's the matter?' asked Kevin, leaning forward.

'Don't know. Just felt a wobble. There it goes again. Think it might be a flat tyre. I'll pull in.'

Mr Blake pulled on the steering wheel, braking gently, and then the car lurched violently, sending them spinning straight across the road. The tyre was not flat: the off-side front wheel careered on down the road leaving the car behind.

The car lay crushed against the sea wall on its off-side, the near-side wheels spinning in the air. Two cars stopped and the drivers ran to help release the occupants. The dog would not stop barking and yelping. He was trembling with fright. Sadie scrambled out first, and then Kevin. They helped to ease out Mr Blake. He was dazed and could not stand. They set him down by the edge of the road. Jack sat beside him licking his face.

By now several other cars had stopped, and soon a police car came along the road. The policeman sent out a call for an ambulance.

'I'm all right,' Mr Blake kept muttering.

'We must have you all checked up,' said the constable.

Sadie and Kevin were bruised and a little shocked but nothing more. Mr Blake had kept his head and controlled the car as far as it was possible so that they had not been travelling very fast when they hit the wall.

'Lucky escape,' said the constable. 'You don't often have much of a chance when a wheel comes off.'

'Can't understand it,' said Mr Blake. 'A wheel coming off.'

'Somebody hasn't tightened it up properly,' said the constable. 'We'll have to check at your garage.'

'Haven't had the wheel changed for months,' said Mr Blake...

They were taken to the nearest hospital by ambulance. The doctor cleared them but stressed that Mr Blake should rest for a few days. 'After all, you're not twenty any longer,' he said. 'You're a bit shaken up. But sound as a bell otherwise.'

Now, using the information in the extract above, write a newspaper article about the incident.

Step 1
Think of a suitable headline for your article. You might also want to include a strap line, which gives a bit more detail about the incident.

Step 2
Decide what factual information you will include in your article. Make a list.

Step 3
Link the actual incident to the general situation in Northern Ireland in the early 1970s. (You may need to research this if you have not already completed the activities in the Conflict in Ireland chapter.)

Step 4
Decide whether you want to include some speculation or opinion in your article and, if so, how you are going to do this.

Step 5
Imagine you interviewed some of the witnesses. Draft some quotations from them to include in your article.

Step 6
Decide what sort of visuals might add interest to your article. Make a list. (If you add a photograph, remember to include a suitable caption.)

Step 7
Plan your article in clearly sequenced paragraphs. Complete a rough first draft.

Step 8
Give your first draft to a partner for their comments. Ask them:
- Does the headline grab your attention?
- Does it give the news in a concise, interesting way?
- As a reader, do you want to know more?
- What are the best aspects of the article?
- Are there any areas that need further work?

Step 9
Re-work your article into a final draft. Remember to proof-read it for punctuation and spelling errors!

Mixed Marriages

1   In areas of conflict life can be very difficult for couples from different backgrounds, particularly if they face resentment and alienation from their families.

The article opposite was written by Martin O'Hagan, and was published in *Fortnight* magazine in June 1986. Read the article and think carefully about the views put forward.

Now answer the following questions on the article.
- What does the phrase 'Running the Gauntlet of Disapproval' mean?
- What does phrase 'mixed marriage' normally mean, and what does it mean in the context of Northern Ireland?
- How do some couples in Northern Ireland try to avoid causing conflict because of their different backgrounds?
- How can mixed marriages affect the education of children?
- Are there any advantages in mixed marriages? (Think about possible long-term effects of increasing tolerance.)

2   In Scene 10, Sadie says, 'I'm not going out with Kevin because he's a Catholic, or a Mick or whatever you want to call him ... I'm going out with him because he's Kevin ... We like being with each other, we don't want to be with anyone else.'

Imagine the story has moved forward in time, and Kevin and Sadie are thinking about getting married, and settling in Northern Ireland. They both want to be together, but are aware of the problems of mixed marriages.

    Write a diary entry for either Sadie or Kevin, in which they write about the issue.

MIXED MARRIAGE – RUNNING THE GAUNTLET OF DISAPPROVAL

In the wake of the recent loyalist gun attack on the Caulfields, MARTIN O'HAGAN talks to couples involved in mixed marriages. And he writes that mixed couples are more readily accepted in Catholic areas but not by the Church.

"THEY SHOOT mixed marriages don't they", Martha said nervously. The Protestant wife of a Craigavon Catholic had just heard the early morning news that loyalist gunmen had murdered Margaret Caulfield, also a Protestant, and seriously wounded her Catholic husband Gerald as the couple lay sleeping in their North Belfast home.

Martha's reaction is indicative of the many people who have married outside their religion and who have run the gauntlet of disapproval from one side or the other. "I felt", she said of the Caulfields, "we had something in common even though we will never meet and now I feel the loss."

The Caulfields had only been married for three weeks at the time of the attack and despite their respective religions, there isn't any suggestion that the couple were practising Christians. They did not appear to be involved politically either. Their only crime was being involved in a 'mixed' marriage and living in a Protestant area.

Strictly speaking mixed marriages are those between a Christian and a non-Christian but in Northern Ireland it means a marriage between a Catholic and a Protestant.

A mixed marriage is often viewed as a betrayal of each other's faith and community and is often actively discouraged by both sides.

Jim, who married a Catholic from the Ormeau Road in Belfast had a 'quiet wedding' because neither set of parents wanted the couple to get married. Since they weren't practising Christians, the couple felt that a wedding in a Registry Office would solve the problems posed by a church wedding especially if it had been a Catholic ceremony. Nevertheless, their only child goes to the local Catholic school because both now live in a Catholic area. Jim feels safer in the area where he thinks there is more tolerance. "But in their own way," he says, "people never let me forget I am an outsider."

Elizabeth, who lives in Portadown's frontline estate of Ballyoran was a Protestant but became a Catholic when she married. She says Protestants are "losing out" because they reject Catholicism and their Irishness. But even after 20 years, Elizabeth says she sometimes still feels like an outsider. She says she stopped children fighting in the street a few months ago and one of them turned and called her "an orange bastard". "They could only have learned that from older people," she says.

Jill, whose baby is over a year old, never had the child baptised because the father, a Catholic, refused to give an undertaking that the child would be reared as a Catholic. Jill's husband believes this is moral blackmail and that strangers "in dog collars have no right to interfere in the running of my family. It's not them who puts bread on our table."

Many mixed couples send their children to integrated and independent schools such as Lagan and Forge. The Catholic Church has steadfastly refused to appoint a chaplain to these schools unlike its Protestant counterpart.

Families who would otherwise have no contact with one another are brought together through a mixed marriage. But after a marriage does little to break the divide. Elizabeth has brothers and sisters living in Protestant areas of Portadown but because of the town's sectarian divisions, they rarely meet. Some of Martha's Protestant relatives will talk to her when they meet on the street but there are others who ignore her.

When Martha's Catholic husband attended the funeral of his father-in-law several years ago, he said he felt unwelcome. He said he was ignored by most of Martha's family and "treated like a leper".

Further Activities

1   Speculate on what might happen to Kevin and Sadie once they have arrived in London, then try writing the outline of a sequel. Note that *Across the Barricades* is the second in a quintet of books about the couple: *The Twelfth of July, Across the Barricades, Into Exile, A Proper Place,* and *Hostages to Fortune.*

2   Produce a programme for a performance of this play. Include a brief summary of the setting and plot, but don't give away the ending!

3   Do some further research about the political situation in Ireland now. Find some newspaper articles and discuss them in small groups.

4   Sketch out a story about another couple who want to be together, despite their different backgrounds, e.g. a Jewish girl and a young Nazi soldier in Germany during the Second World War.

OXFORD Playscripts

Across the Barricades; Joan Lingard, adapted by David Ian Neville

Dracula; Bram Stoker, adapted by David Calcutt

Brother in the Land; Robert Swindells, adapted by Joe Standerline

Dr Faustus; Christopher Marlowe, adapted by Geraldine McCaughrean

Johnny and the Dead; Terry Pratchett, adapted by Stephen Briggs

Frankenstein; Mary Shelley, adapted by Philip Pullman

The Amazing Maurice and his Educated Rodents; Terry Pratchett, adapted by Stephen Briggs

Lady Macbeth; David Calcutt

The Snake-stone; adapted from her own novel by Berlie Doherty

The Valley of Fear; Arthur Conan Doyle, adapted by Adrian Flynn

The Turbulent Term of Tyke Tiler; adapted from her own novel by Gene Kemp

Troy 24; David Calcutt

The Demon Headmaster; Gillian Cross, adapted by Adrian Flynn

The White Rose and the Swastika; Adrian Flynn

The Canterbury Tales; Geoffrey Chaucer, adapted by Martin Riley

Salem; David Calcutt

For more information or to request your inspection copy of any of the Playscripts titles, please call customer services on +44 (0) 1536 741068